WONDERS OF MAN

KYOTO

by Edwin Bayrd

and the Editors
of the Newsweek Book Division

NEWSWEEK, New York

NEWSWEEK BOOK DIVISION

JOSEPH L. GARDNER	*Editor*
Janet Czarnetzki	*Art Director*
Jonathan Bartlett	*Associate Editor*
Laurie P. Winfrey	*Picture Editor*
Kathleen Berger	*Copy Editor*
S. ARTHUR DEMBNER	*Publisher*

WONDERS OF MAN

MILTON GENDEL	*Consulting Editor*
Mary Ann Joulwan	*Designer, Kyoto*

Endpapers:
*In this seventeenth-century view of
Kyoto, pagoda and palace alike are
swaddled in dense clouds of gold.*

Title page:
Vermilion torii, *donated by worshipers,
overarch the approach to Fushimi Inari,
one of Kyoto's oldest Shinto shrines.*

Opposite:
*Kakiemon ware, with its graceful lines
and vibrant overglazes, was to prove a
highly popular export after the opening
of Japan to Western trade in 1854.*

ISBN: Clothbound Edition 0–88225–085–X
ISBN: Deluxe Edition 0–88225–086–8
Library of Congress Catalog Card No. 73–87150
© 1974 — Arnoldo Mondadori Editore, S.p.A.
All rights reserved. Printed and bound in Italy.

Contents

Introduction

Kyoto, capital of Japan for fully half that nation's recorded history, is actually many cities in one. It is the metropolis founded in A.D. 794 by Emperor Kammu, a city of rectilinear streets and brilliantly lacquered pagodas. It is the home of Genji, the "shining prince" of Lady Murasaki's epic eleventh-century romance, a city of cloistered palaces and graceful country temples. It is the last refuge of the nation's fading aristocracy, a city of gilded pleasure domes and rustic tea pavilions. It is the disputed prize of Japan's great feudal period, a city of moated castles and sumptuous baronial residences. It is the cultural capital of a willfully isolationist archipelago, a city of tranquil Zen Buddhist gardens like Daisen-in (left) and elegant princely villas. And it is, perhaps most significantly of all, a thriving modern city that incorporates and preserves elements of each of its earlier identities.

In that sense, Kyoto is a kind of vast, open-air archive of Japanese art and architecture, a tangible testament — written in timber and granite, lacquer and gilt, rice paper and bamboo — to a millennium of imperial history. Its attractions are manifold, its appeal legendary, and its variety infinite. There are more than two thousand temples and shrines in Kyoto, ranging in size from Higashi Hongan-ji, capped by the largest wooden roof in the world, to Gio-ji, whose total floor area does not exceed two hundred square feet. Each of these sites has its champions, and each of those champions has his own set of preferences and preconceptions. Indeed, it is often said that there are as many views of Kyoto as there are visitors to the ancient imperial capital each year — and that number now exceeds 33 million annually.

THE EDITORS

11

KYOTO IN HISTORY

I

Purple Hills and Crystal Streams

By Western count, the year was A.D. 800, the year of Charlemagne's coronation. By Japanese count, it was Enryaku 19, the nineteenth full year in the reign of Kammu, the fiftieth emperor of the island kingdom. In the West, the year was marked by a nine-month-long royal progress that traversed most of Frankland and terminated in Rome in late November. There, on Christmas Day, the conqueror of Italy, Spain, and Germany accepted the crown of the Holy Roman Empire, thus becoming the spiritual as well as the temporal master of Western Europe. In the East, the year 800 marked the official completion of Japan's magnificent new imperial capital. In the shadow of Mount Hiei, a sprawling and resplendent metropolis had risen under Emperor Kammu's aegis, a city that he called Heian-kyō, Capital of Peace and Tranquillity. That official designation never became popular, however, and later generations knew the city by a succession of other names — Miyako, Raku, Rakuyō. Ultimately it would be known as Kyoto, a name derived from two Chinese characters signifying "capital."

Viewed from Mount Hiei, ninth-century Heian-kyō was most unprepossessing — a vast parallelogram cross-hatched by intersecting avenues and composed almost entirely of single-story buildings roofed with tile, shingle, or thatch. From the city's southern gate the impression was altogether different, however, for from that point Heian-kyō's great central boulevard, Suzaku-ōji, stretched die-straight northward to the gates of the imperial enclosure, some two and a half miles distant. From this vantage, Heian-kyō's symmetry was absolute, its scale monumental, and its effect both calculated and immediate. Its grand geometry dwarfed the visitor, and

its sweep accentuated the remoteness of the emperor, spiritual and temporal master of the Japanese people.

The year 800 was one of high promise in Western Europe as well as in Japan, for in both places years of factionalism and strife seemed at last to be giving way to a new and more stable order. Unhappily for the subject peoples of Western Europe, that promise was to dim with Charlemagne's death in 814 and disappear for a millennium in the internecine feuding that followed. Happily for the people of Kammu's kingdom, the great capital that he established in the mist-shrouded foothills of Hiei not only survived the emperor but grew with a vigor and speed that might have astonished its founder. Within a century of Kammu's death, Heian-kyō could justifiably claim to be the second most important center of culture in the entire world, surpassed only by the Chinese capital of Ch'ang-an — the city upon which Heian-kyō was openly modeled.

Japan's evolution from primitive agrarianism to aristocratic bureaucracy during this period represented the culmination of a process that actually began fully a thousand years before the founding of Heian-kyō, for it was then that the cultural traits so closely associated with the Japanese people — political insularity, social rigidity, religious tolerance, and intense clan loyalty — began to develop. Those traits, which manifested themselves dramatically in the personality of Kammu, were characteristics common to his people, making him less a shaper of history in the Carolingian mold than the embodiment of centuries of cultural transformation.

According to the annals of the Japanese imperial family, which claims the oldest unbroken dynastic line in the world, those years of transformation began in

660 B.C., the year traditionally assigned to the accession of Jimmu Tennō, the legendary first emperor of Japan. Archaeologists have probed tens of thousands of years deeper into the Japanese past, however, and their findings point to the existence of a culture on the islands at least 100,000 years ago. At that time the Japanese archipelago was joined to the Asian mainland by a series of land bridges, but by Neolithic times the islands lay some one hundred miles from the tip of the Korean peninsula (see map, page 66). This geographic isolation helps explain the relatively late settlement of the archipelago in prehistoric times — and also the extraordinary homogeneity of the Japanese people in modern times.

The southern islands of Kyushu and Shikoku were to prove a fertile seedbed for migrant civilizations once the treacherous Korean Strait had been crossed, but for eons that gulf would loom broad and impassable. In fact, it seems likely that the islands were first settled by Asian immigrants driven east by pressures that an increasingly vigorous China was exerting along the periphery of its empire. Subsequent waves of migrants included proto-Negroid ancestors of the Malay, New Guinea, and Filipino peoples; proto-Caucasoids, from whom the aboriginal Ainu of Japan's northern islands are presumed to be descended; and, finally, a dominant group of Mongoloids who carried with them a sophisticated bronze and iron culture from the plains of inner Asia. Despite later infusions of Chinese, Korean, and Southeast Asian stock, there can be little question that it was these Mongoloids who established the first Japanese state, for it is their distinctive artifacts — the sword, the comma-shaped

jewels known as *magatama,* and the bronze ritual mirror — that have been recognized through the centuries as symbols of imperial authority.

After 4500 B.C. there is increasing evidence of settled civilization, located in the southern and central regions of Japan. Shell middens, sunken pit dwellings, stone tools, and other relics — all dating from this period — have been found in profusion, but it is pottery of a highly sophisticated and almost baroque style that hallmarks the age. Indeed, that pottery, distinguished by its cord-marked design, or *jōmon,* has given a name to the first epoch in Japan's Neolithic history.

In the third century B.C., Jōmon culture was disrupted by the sudden appearance of a new and radically advanced wave of immigrants, the Yayoi, whose name is associated with an equally distinctive but far more austere style of pottery. Possibly driven from the mainland by the dynastic wars that attended the unification of China under the Ch'in and Han, these settlers rapidly displaced the Jōmon. So complete was this takeover that the Jōmon virtually disappeared as a cultural force, making the Yayoi the true ancestral culture of Japan. This Yayoi influx, which brought with it the advanced rice culture of the continent, also introduced the techniques of metalsmithing, animal husbandry, spinning, and bronze casting to Japan, hastening the country's conversion to a fully agrarian economy.

A distinctive feature of the Yayoi period, which lasted roughly from 200 B.C. to A.D. 200, was the evolution of pronounced social stratification and particularly of clan organization, the kinship-based focus of traditional Japanese society. In a sense, such stratification was a logical outgrowth of the Yayoi invasion, for as

Japan's earliest Neolithic age takes its name from the distinctive pottery produced by the archipelago's first inhabitants. Cordlike markings known as jōmon *indicate that the graceful footed bowl at left was shaped and fired during the first millennium* B.C. *Surviving works of the late Jōmon period — among them the flame-capped earthenware vessel at right — suggest a culture of remarkable inventiveness.*

the food supply became more stable and the population more sedentary, the topography of the land itself became increasingly important. Japan's numerous mountain vales and readily irrigated plains favored compartmentalization into small, self-contained communities — and this in turn fostered an intensification of individual tribal loyalties.

By the end of the Yayoi period, Japanese society had coalesced into distinct clan units, many of which were already beginning the process of amalgamation that would eventually unify them under the leadership of the imperial clan. Chinese emissaries traveling in Kyushu in the third century A.D. noted the proliferation of what they termed "countries" — the distinct territorial holdings of local tribes and clans. By this time marked gradations of rank were already observable within these clans, and a distinct hierarchy was emerging, with society dividing into two interacting social entities: the *uji*, or clan proper, and the *be*, or guild. The former were composed of households that claimed common ancestry, had a common chieftain, and worshiped a common guardian deity; the latter were formed of subservient household communities associated through some common mode of service to the clans. These occupational groups constituted the bulk of the population, while the *uji* formed a loose aristocracy. *Uji* chieftains, who claimed descent from their clans' guardian deities, wielded ritual as well as social power — a fusion of sacerdotal and secular duties that was integral to the development of the state. In fact, the belief that government and cultic ritual were but two aspects of the same function — and therefore justifiably administered by one person — was so deeply in-

grained in the Japanese nature that it endured well into the twentieth century.

During the Yayoi period there existed a wide diversity of clan cults, but over the ensuing centuries those various rituals gradually fused into a body of uniform belief, one that would ultimately become known as Shinto, the state religion of Japan. This indigenous cult was by no means a complex religious system, for it stemmed in large measure from a primitive attunement to natural forces, which the early Japanese identified as immanent deities, or *kami*. From very early times, the people of Japan clearly felt a collective kinship with nature — and, by extension, with the particular deities believed to inhabit every aspect of the concrete world. Cultic ritual centered upon the rejection of all that threatened to taint or defile the sacredness attached to particular localities and their indwelling spirits, and this in turn fostered a respect for the legitimacy of previously established authority.

Government, at least of a national sort, was nonexistent during the early Yayoi period, but in the third century A.D. a clan chieftain from the south — later identified with the mythic emperor Jimmu — led an expedition northeast out of Kyushu to establish a new base of power in the Yamato region of central Honshu. This epic migration brought the first settled government to the north shore of the Inland Sea. These "men of Yamato," possessing a superior Iron Age culture, were able to subdue and unify the weaker indigenous clans in their path and establish a vague suzerainty over central and western Japan. Their domination of the Yamato region was apparently achieved through coalition and conciliation as well as force of arms, and

their ascendancy was marked by the sudden appearance of monumental earthen burial mounds whose dimensions were unprecedented.

It has been suggested that the *kofun*, or "tomb," culture of the Yamato region is proof of the sudden influx of yet another vigorous foreign culture, but it is more likely that the Kofun era was merely an evolutionary phase of Yayoi, albeit enriched by continental contact. Whatever the case, the artifacts of the Kofun period undeniably represent a major cultural advance. According to the Tokyo-born American historian John Whitney Hall, these tombs clearly reveal "a class of warrior aristocrats who possessed the power to rule over a thickly settled countryside and to draw upon the agricultural produce of the regions they controlled." Perhaps more significantly, the Kofun tombs suggest a high degree of social organization, for it is clear that their building required both skilled and unskilled labor in great quantities and significant sources of revenue.

Kofun tombs took several forms, the most distinctive of which was the keyhole shape. The burial chamber itself contained not only the remains of a great Yamato chieftain, but also innumerable bronze funerary objects of Chinese origin. Set into the sloping sides of the mound itself were rows of pottery cylinders capped by small terra-cotta figures, known as *haniwa*, whose Mongoloid features suggest their creators' Asian origins.

That Yamato chieftains, Japan's first true sovereigns, should choose to be entombed with venerated objects of Chinese origin is not particularly surprising, for cultural borrowing from China had been taking place in a slow and largely unconscious manner for centuries. By the time the Great Wall was completed, northern

Around the third century B.C. a boldly assertive new group of immigrants from the mainland settled in Japan, displacing the indigenous Jōmon. These socially and technologically sophisticated newcomers, the Yayoi, introduced a completely different pottery (upper left), characterized by fluid lines and lack of ornamentation. They were also to create the extraordinary tomb figurines known as haniwa — *the most primitive of which come from the Kyoto area, where the enormous earthen burial mounds of Japan's earliest emperors are to be found. Later examples include the house at left, the stylized dancers shown above, and the horse at right.*

The formal introduction of Buddhism into Japan in the sixth century A.D. *precipitated a new epoch of artistic expression. As enthusiasm for the faith grew, native artists and artisans in ever-increasing numbers turned their talents to glorifying the new religion. A typical product of the period is this Buddhist banner, whose filigreed bronze medallions fall in shimmering cascades from a panel of the same material. According to popular belief, a worshiper had only to brush his head against the banner to achieve a state of perfect grace.*

Korea was already an established outpost of Chinese civilization, and by the first century A.D. bronze ritual mirrors, lacquerware, and gold filigreework of continental design had begun to appear in Japan, indicating growing commercial contact across the Korean Strait. Chinese court annals of the period record that a small Japanese delegation reached the imperial court at Loyang in A.D. 57, by which time Chinese and Koreans had begun to settle in Japan. This pattern of influence — first goods, then colonists — was perhaps inevitable, for the Japanese hunger for Chinese objects was matched or surpassed by a hunger for Chinese ideas. Refugees from the mainland were welcomed in the Yamato region, and the "men of Han" who settled there in the fourth and fifth centuries were integrated into the Japanese clan system. The *aya-be,* or brocade-makers' guild, was composed exclusively of Chinese émigrés, and Chinese scribes and accountants, whose skills were held in awe by the unlettered Japanese, formed an aristocracy based not so much on kinship but on literacy.

By the close of the fifth century, Japan had officially adopted Chinese ideograms in the absence of a written language of its own. That decision, made in ignorance, was extremely ill-advised, for written Chinese characters, each of which represented a single object, action, or concept, bore no relation whatsoever to spoken Japanese. Chinese was monosyllabic, tonal, abstract, and isolative; Japanese, by contrast, was polysyllabic, phonetic, virtually unaccented, and hampered by a long and diffuse sentence structure. Early attempts to equate Chinese characters with Japanese syllables were both awkward and haphazard, and it was several centuries

before the written language was formalized. The end product, a cumbersome combination of the two, would force generations of Japanese into rote work of stupefying tediousness in order to master what Edwin O. Reischauer, another Tokyo-born American historian, has called the least efficient language system in wide use anywhere in the world.

The misguided decision to adopt Chinese ideograms was logical in its context, however, for it came at the beginning of the era of wholesale borrowing from China. Over the next two centuries the Japanese would also adopt Chinese systems of land distribution, taxation, civil administration, court protocol, and religious observance. The first and most sweeping of these intellectual imports was the practice of Buddhism, traditionally said to have reached Japan in A.D. 552. Buddhism had in fact been known in Japan for some time, but its emergence as a vitally important cultural force clearly dates from the sixth century. It was a time of political consolidation and centralization, which may account for the enormous appeal that Buddhism — a unified, centrally controlled state religion — eventually came to exert upon the populace.

In the beginning there were, perhaps inevitably, clashes between those factions favoring acceptance of the new religion and those cleaving to the Shinto pantheon. In 552, the ruler of Paekche, one of the rival kingdoms of southern Korea, presented a gilt bronze image of the Buddha to Japan's emperor. Concerned that the worship of a foreign idol might anger the native tutelary gods, the emperor entrusted the statue to the care of the prominent Soga clan, who found Buddhism a powerful and effective tool in their campaign

to restructure the archaic legitimization of imperial authority. The determination of the Soga to seize control of the state eventually led to civil war and regicide — and by 587 the pro-Buddhist faction, under Soga leadership, had effectively cleared the way for a rapid importation of continental ideas. Their victory was one of minor military consequence but incalculable historical import, for it was the philosophical stimulus of Buddhism, as much as any other factor, that spurred the national impulse to learning.

At this time it was the custom to abandon the imperial palace — and frequently the capital itself — upon the death of an emperor, an extravagant gesture doubtless derived from ancient Shinto purification rituals. As the court grew larger and more unwieldy, and architecture became more permanent, these moves decreased in both frequency and range, and during the century that followed the introduction of Buddhism to Japan the court remained in the vicinity of Asuka, near modern Nara. In that interval at least forty-six major Buddhist temples were erected; foremost among them was Hōryū-ji, a Chinese-style temple and monastery founded in 607 by Prince Regent Shōtoku. The Kondō, or Golden Hall, of Hōryū-ji is, without question, the oldest wooden structure in the world, having survived by many centuries the last of the T'ang dynasty temples whose design it imitates.

No historical figure more completely personifies the spirit of this era of enthusiastic and unalloyed imitation of China than Prince Regent Shōtoku, whose father, Emperor Yōmei, was Japan's first avowedly Buddhist monarch. The earliest extant histories of Japan identify Shōtoku as the author of commentaries on

21

Buddhist scripture, as the commissioner of the nation's
first official historical record, and as the promulgator
of the first constitution. This last, a seventeen-article
list of moral injunctions in the Confucian mode, can
hardly be termed a legal code, but it does clearly enun-
ciate a concept borrowed directly from China — the
theory of an all-powerful centralized state.

Stories relating to the exploits of Prince Shōtoku
exist in such abundance that it is often difficult to separate fact from reverent legend. The portrait that does
consistently emerge from these accounts is that of a
political career entirely dedicated to the task of raising
the level of Japanese civilization and thereby securing
prestige both at home and abroad. The reforms that
Shōtoku sponsored — from the adoption of the Chinese
calendar to the importation of the continental Buddhist church — were all directed to this end.

If only half the accomplishments that have been attributed to Prince Shōtoku are true, he still remains
Japan's first great historical figure. It was at his instigation, for instance, that a major embassy set out for
China in 607. They bore greetings "from the ruler of
the land where the sun rises to the ruler of the land
where the sun sets." And presumptuous as that saluta-
tion was, it did suggest the degree to which Japan's national consciousness had evolved in a single century of
Chinese influence.

Unfortunately, Shōtoku's death in 622 brought with
it a resumption of the clan warfare that had plagued
the nation since the introduction of Buddhism. This
bitter and divisive political jockeying continued for
a generation, ending in 645 only through the concerted
efforts of a Yamato court clique committed to a policy

Nara, Japan's first permanent capital, was a city dominated by Buddhist monasteries, the most grandiose of which was Tōdai-ji. The architectural and spiritual heart of that complex was the Daibutsu-den (left), built to house a monumental cast bronze Buddha weighing more than 550 tons. Both building and statue were unprecedented in size, and their construction nearly emptied the imperial family's coffers. Providentially, a rich vein of gold was discovered nearby as the project neared completion, making it possible to sheathe the temple's central image (right) with a quarter ton of gilt.

of Sinicizing Japan. Students recently returned from the mainland — among them members of Shōtoku's embassy of 607 — formed an important element of this clique, which was determined to break the power of the clans through a dramatic reallocation of power.

On paper, the laws drawn up between 645–50 and known as the Taika ("Great Change") Reform were both radical and inflexible. They proposed nothing less than a new system of land tenure, local government, and national taxation, all based upon T'ang precedents. In practice, these reforms, which were formulized half a century later as part of the Taihō Code of 702, were rather circumscribed. Their purpose was the redistribution of economic as well as political power — and that goal was achieved at the expense of the peasants. To them fell the largest burden of taxation, with the smallest concomitant rewards.

T'ang China's highly refined system of land distribution and taxation — a bureaucratic system whose complexity is almost unrivaled in human history — worked on the mainland only with repeated modification, and then only with sporadic success. It was distinctly ill-suited to the clan-ridden Japanese state, which took over the forms and even the terminology of the T'ang bureaucratic system without inculcating its fundamental principles. The result was a strict aristocracy of birth rather than merit, entrenched, inefficient, and foredoomed — although few eighth-century observers could have guessed as much.

The first tangible, large-scale manifestation of the transfer of Chinese institutions to Japanese soil came in 710 with the foundation of Japan's first permanent capital, Nara. An idealized model of the T'ang capital of Ch'ang-an, the new city was rectilinear in layout, and although the population of the region was never sufficient to settle the western half of the city, great boulevards were laid out in that direction to preserve the symmetry favored by Chinese geomancers.

The Nara period (710–84) has been labeled the golden age of Buddhist art in Japan — which is to say a conservative reflection of T'ang art transmuted by Japanese sensibility, for at the time Japan had no real religious art of its own. The native Shinto cult was in fact distinguished by its near-total lack of plastic or graphic art; the myriad deities with which the Japanese cosmos was peopled were deemed too abstract or mysterious to be represented iconographically. It was a period of prodigious output during which a number of great monasteries were either erected in Nara or transferred there, timber by timber, from other sites. Their function was two-fold: to embellish the new capital, and to throw a magical cordon around it to ward off malign influences. Paramount among these complexes was Tōdai-ji, set in a two-mile-square enclosure in the eastern sector of the new capital. The monastery's great hall, originally 284 feet long and half again as high, is the largest wooden building ever constructed under one roof, which makes it an appropriate setting for the enormous Buddha that sits in its central hall.

The great copper, tin, and lead Buddha of Tōdai-ji weighs more than a million pounds and stands fifty-three feet high, but it is the statue's remarkable history as much as its incredible bulk that merits consideration, for its creation represented a critical step in the reconciliation of Shinto and Buddhist factions. Although conceived by Emperor Shōmu in 735 — in part to com-

Japan's first official contact with mainland China came in A.D. 57, when a small embassy reached the court of the Han dynasty emperor Kuang-wu. To commemorate that occasion, the Chinese emperor ordered a special gold signet struck and presented to the foreigners. The impression (left) created by that seal bestows vassalage rank upon a ruler of the Yayoi people. By the eighth century, contacts between the two countries had broadened to include clerics and craftsmen (below), as well as official envoys. And by the time Kyoto was founded in 794, the impact of mainland culture was everywhere in evidence: the new imperial palace was Chinese in style, and Chinese-style artworks such as the bronze ornament opposite decorated local temples.

As the diagram below indicates, tenth-century Kyoto — which was officially known as Heian-kyō, or Capital of Peace and Tranquillity — was a neat parallelogram enclosing two large temple precincts and the vast Daidairi, or imperial enclosure. The gardens of Shinsen-en, which encircled the southern walls of the Daidairi, also encompassed the city's university, a center of Chinese learning.

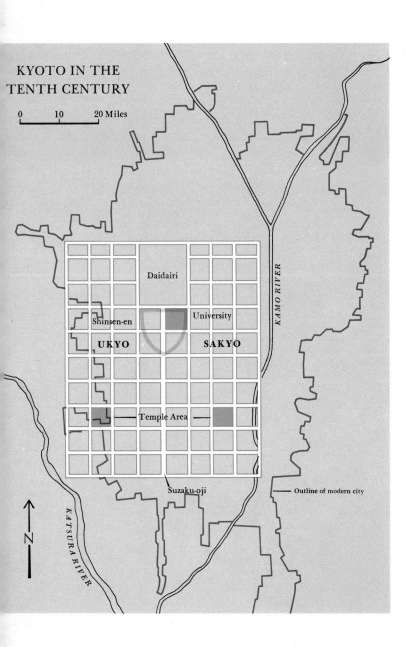

KYOTO IN THE
TENTH CENTURY

0   10   20 Miles

Daidairi

KAMO RIVER

Shinsen-en   University

UKYO   SAKYO

Temple Area

Suzaku-oji   —— Outline of modern city

N

KATSURA RIVER

memorate the city's deliverance from a smallpox epidemic and in part to consolidate Shōmu's own position as spiritual chief of state — the project lay dormant for almost a decade. Unable to inspire the populace to contribute funds for the statue's construction, the emperor turned in desperation to the monk Gyōgi, whose unorthodox teachings had won him few friends at court but a sizable popular following. Legend has it that Gyōgi inaugurated a highly successful fund-raising campaign by undertaking a pilgrimage to the nation's most sacred Shinto shrine, at Ise, where he presented a Buddhist relic as an offering. Thereafter, donations poured into Tōdai-ji from the followers of both religions. At a somewhat later date, a Shinto emblem from Kyushu was enshrined at Tōdai-ji, and subsequently every major Buddhist temple was constructed under the guardianship of a local Shinto shrine.

The Nara period also produced Japan's first formal literature, among which were two quasi-historical annals known as the *Kojiki* ("Records of Ancient Matters") and the *Nihon-shoki* ("Chronicles of Japan"). The former, commissioned two years after the founding of Nara, is thought by some to be a surviving draft of the latter, which was written in 720, for the two treat roughly the same sequence of events. Each work draws upon traditional legend cycles in order to document a glorified history of the men of Yamato. Modeled upon the court annals of T'ang China — and written in a combination of Chinese and archaic Japanese — these histories attempted to legitimize the ascendancy of the Yamato clan by recasting early Japanese history in a boldly fictive vein. From this date, the imperial family would claim descent not merely from the warrior chieftains who settled the Yamato in the third century A.D., but from the legendary Jimmu Tennō himself, said to have ruled nearly a millennium earlier. And through Jimmu they would trace their lineage directly back to Amaterasu, goddess of the sun.

Four divinely descended emperors and three empresses would rule Nara over the next three-quarters of a century, a period of mounting civil unrest and widespread political corruption. An imperial edict issued by Emperor Kōnin in 775 laments: "It has come to our ears that, while the functionaries at the capital are poorly paid and cannot escape the hardships of cold and hunger, provincial governors make great profits." His words seem to suggest that the centralized administrative system was already breaking down. The throne was under attack by rapacious and power-hungry Buddhist monks — whose ascendancy over a succession of female sovereigns had dangerously undermined imperial authority — and the empire was plagued by incessant intrigues. Therefore, Kōnin's successor, Emperor Kammu, boldly attempted to escape both challenges by moving the capital thirty miles northwest to Nagaoka.

The transfer, ordered by Kammu in 784, the third year of his reign, was both costly and hurried. The emperor himself resettled in the new capital after six months, but the court did not follow for several years. During that time the entire country's tax revenues were funneled into Nagaoka, where bridges, roads, and temples were constructed under the able supervision of a Fujiwara clansman named Tanetsugu. An industrious and well-organized royal overseer, Tanetsugu acquitted himself well in Kammu's eyes, but not without making powerful enemies at court, among them Crown Prince Sawara and members of a number of rival clans. At their instigation, a rumor was broadcast that a family of Chinese descent had ceded the land upon which the new capital was rising in exchange for certain unspecified favors. The scandal eventually tainted the apparently innocent Tanetsugu, whose resultant fall from favor culminated in his assassination in 785. This tragic incident provided his clansmen, the Fujiwara, with all the excuse they needed for a concerted attack upon their rivals, and a series of arrests and executions followed. The chief conspirators were sent into exile, but Prince Sawara never reached his destination, an island in the Inland Sea, and many in the capital assumed that he had been murdered en route. Coincidentally, the Fujiwara clan and the imperial family suffered a series of grave personal misfortunes — which the superstitious populace lost no time in blaming upon the vengeful spirit of the crown prince.

To placate Prince Sawara's wrathful spirit, the government took the extraordinary step of posthumously proclaiming him emperor. Kammu took the additional precaution of abandoning the accursed capital and resettling ten miles to the northwest in the village of Uda, which the emperor renamed Heian-kyō. The spot Kammu had chosen was singularly lovely, its natural beauty a distinct contrast to the undistinguished plains upon which the two previous capitals had risen. Later generations would confirm the wisdom of Kammu's decision by dubbing Heian-kyō the city of "purple hills and crystal streams." In April 793, on the advice of royal geomancers, the outlines of the new capital were laid out between the Katsura River on the west and the Kamo on the east, and a year later the city began to take shape within these boundaries (see diagram, page 28). To economize, many buildings in Nagaoka were simply disassembled and transferred to the new site, there to be reconstructed along an identical gridwork of intersecting avenues.

Heian-kyō's long axis ran three and a third miles north-south, its east-west axis was roughly half a mile shorter, and like Nara and Nagaoka it adhered to the strict geometry of Ch'ang-an. The city's magnificent axial way was lined with the mansions of powerful aristocrats, government offices, subsidiary palaces, and numerous civic institutions, foremost among them the university, which adjoined the south gate of the imperial enclosure itself. The Daidairi, as the royal enclave was known, was centered along the city's north wall. It measured almost three-quarters of a mile across, and extended a full mile south into the city itself. A thirty-three-acre pleasure garden, the Shinsen-en, curved protectively around the southern end of the Daidairi, further isolating the emperor and his retinue.

The Daidairi's fourteen major gates opened onto a labyrinthine complex of imperial apartments, ceremonial pavilions, and great halls of state. Many of these were rich in detailing and elegant in their appointments, but none surpassed the Daigoku-den, or Great Hall of State. An early description notes:

It stood on a stone platform, guarded by red lacquered balustrades, and consisted of a hall about 170 feet long and 50 feet wide, under a roof supported by 52 pillars. The whole was painted red, and the roof was of emerald blue tiles. In the centre of the hall stood, on a raised platform under a canopy surmounted by golden phoenixes, the Imperial Throne.

This royal audience hall, like the other buildings of the Daidairi — and like the great mansions, government offices, and tradesmen's houses that lay beyond — was constructed almost entirely of wood, and consequently it was especially susceptible to the twin curses of fire and earthquake. Indeed, the unfinished capital was severely damaged by a series of strong earth tremors only three years after its founding, and others would strike sporadically throughout the city's history. Fire, a more frequent and more fearsome foe, would consume Heian-kyō's dry timbers and musty thatch with awesome regularity and almost uncheckable voracity over the years. A flash fire did extensive damage to the Daigoku-den in 876, for example, and a great holocaust reduced half the city to ashes in 960.

Add to these elemental forces the destructive impact of successive civil wars, many waged in the streets of the capital itself, and it is little wonder that nothing survives of ninth-century Heian-kyō — no temples, no palaces, no halls of state. Nothing, that is, except a fragment of Shinsen-en, the pleasure garden that Emperor Kammu first toured in the year of Charlemagne's triumph. Reduced to little more than a two-acre duck pond, the park bears scant resemblance to the magnificent gardens that once extended both north and south of it. Indeed, Shinsen-en's very survival has been attributed not to its beauties, which are neglible, but to its practicality as a central source of water for fire fighting and irrigation. Yet for whatever reason, it has endured, serene and neglected, in the heart of the modern city — a fraction of the whole, and a touchstone for any study of the ancient capital's long, turbulent, and colorful history.

*Fires, earthquakes, and marauding armies have all
but obliterated Shinsen-en, the fabulous pleasure
garden that once adjoined the palace of Emperor
Kammu, Kyoto's founder. Only the duck pond
remains (below) — and its existence owes more to
pragmatism than to sentiment, for its waters were
used to fight the flash fires that plagued Kammu's
capital. In time those flames were to consume every
one of the original city's wood and thatch structures.*

II

Dwellers Among the Clouds

Emperor Kammu's legacy was a mixed one at best. The state system that he bequeathed to his successors encouraged cultural evolution on a heretofore unprecedented scale, while at the same time nurturing elements that would divide and ultimately dissolve the system itself. Indeed, at the time of Kammu's death in A.D. 806, the aristocrats of Heian-kyō had already settled upon a course of social and political action that would permit their privileged numbers to dwell in elegant isolation while the rest of the country slowly reverted to patterns of clan rule that had, at least in theory, been supplanted in 702 by the Taihō Code.

The abrogation of that code, which had provided for the establishment of a strong central government and a national system of taxation and land distribution, was almost imperceptibly gradual — and frequently unintentional. When, for example, Emperor Kammu issued a series of edicts designed to revise the process of tax collection set forth in the code, he was merely attempting to bolster the court's revenue-gathering capacity. The cumulative effect of these revisions was precisely the opposite, however. The emperor's authority to levy and collect taxes was formalized by the code, and once that authority had been compromised — even by the emperor himself — the court's ability to exact revenues began to diminish by slow and seemingly irreversible degrees.

In the first decades of his reign Kammu moved with equal boldness to eradicate the perennial threat posed by the Ainu, the indigenous tribesmen whose periodic raids had plagued the government throughout the Nara period. In 812, after an intermittent campaign lasting more than ten years, the Ainu were finally de-feated by Funya no Watamaro, a brilliant field commander who bore the title of *sei-i tai shōgun,* or "barbarian-subduing generalissimo." Watamaro's title was honorific, of course, but warriors who gained the title in subsequent centuries were to make the shogunate into the supreme political office in the nation, expropriating powers once exercised by the emperor.

By the same token, Kammu's determination to disestablish church and state in Heian-kyō was to have unforeseen and ultimately tragic ramifications. By restricting all temple-building in the new capital to two small and carefully circumscribed areas in the city's southern quadrants, the emperor hoped to isolate the contentious Buddhist monks whose power had come to rival that of the crown itself. So restricted, the temples of Heian-kyō could never pose a direct threat to imperial authority, as the great monasteries of Nara had, and in that sense at least Kammu's decree achieved its desired effect. The Buddhist centers in the capital never approached Tōdai-ji or Hōryū-ji in size or impact; instead, new centers of Buddhist power arose on the city's outskirts, principally on Mount Hiei. Kammu encouraged this development initially, seeing in it a means of breaking the still-considerable power of the Nara priesthood. The emperor's successors would find this legacy two-sided, however, for the bellicose clerics of Hiei soon turned upon their benefactors. For centuries thereafter these warrior-monks bullied and blackmailed the helpless imperial household, leading the twelfth-century emperor Go-Shirakawa to exclaim: "There are three things that I cannot control: the fall of the dice, the flow of the river Kamo, and the turbulent monks of Mount Hiei."

In at least one other important respect the capital's later troubles can be traced back to Kammu's time, for it was he who firmly established the royal practice of granting *shōen*, or tax-exempt provincial manors, to imperial favorites — a further subversion of the Taihō Code. Faced with the prospect of housing the enormous and ever-growing imperial family, Kammu prudently decreed that all princes below the fourth rank in the court hierarchy should be demoted to noble, but nonroyal, status and awarded *shōen* in the provinces. This, too, proved to be a wrongheaded solution to a real and pressing problem, for although Kammu's systematic pruning of the imperial tree did reduce the number of headstrong, power-hungry young men at court, it also planted potential political rivals in every corner of the realm. In time, these lateral branches of the imperial clan would return to court, not to claim the throne but to rule from behind it. Under new family names derived from the locales in which they had settled, they would reclaim their birthright by proxy, governing Japan through their military prowess.

These years of gradual economic decline and steady political usurpation were also years of unparalleled cultural attainment, and it is for these achievements that the Heian period is extolled today as the golden age of Japanese history. Isolated by circumstance and insular by choice, the Heian court endured for almost four centuries in a kind of hermetic splendor, far removed from the realities of provincial existence. During those centuries the court was to transfigure totally the alien Chinese culture that it had enthusiastically embraced during the Nara period — thus completing one cycle in the pattern of acquisition, assimilation, and selective improvisation that is the most distinctive feature of Japan's cultural history. Under the influence of Kammu's successors and their powerful first ministers, the Fujiwara, Heian-kyō was to become the nation's first truly Japanese city. Nara would sink back into provincial obscurity, and the dismantled capital of Nagaoka would be returned to rice cultivation, but Heian-kyō would thrive for a millennium and more — a testament to both the vitality and the vision of the imperial capital's early leaders.

The emergence of a vigorous, sophisticated, and independent Japanese culture — a phenomenon of the first half of the ninth century — was clearly related to the decline of the T'ang dynasty on the mainland. The final dissolution of the T'ang did not come until 907, but by that time the dynasty had been moribund for a century and a half. The coup d'etat engineered by the rebel general An Lu-shan in 755 had failed to extinguish the T'ang line, but it had dealt the dynasty a blow from which it never fully recovered, and from that time China's overseas influence declined steadily. Japan's reaction was, understandably, a delayed one, filtered as it was through Korea, but by the time Heian-kyō was founded the number of annual missions to China had dropped appreciably. By 838, when the last official embassy departed for the T'ang court, the Japanese were openly weighing the hazards of the crossing against the benefits that might be derived from it. Those benefits were obviously judged to be slim, for the contingent returned to Heian-kyō less than a year later, and future embassies were canceled.

As early as the mid-ninth century, subtle Japanese modifications of the traditional Chinese city plan were

The Heian Shrine, constructed in 1894 to celebrate the eleven-hundredth anniversary of Kyoto's founding, includes a scaled-down replica of the Daigoku-den, Emperor Kammu's great hall of state. The perfect lateral symmetry and bold color scheme of the hall and its long flanking pavilions (right) reveal the extent to which eighth-century Japanese architects were influenced by Chinese design.

in evidence throughout Heian-kyō, concrete reflections of a reassessment of T'ang ideals and institutions. The familiar gridwork pattern remained, but its lateral symmetry had already begun to break down. As originally laid out, the city's central boulevard, Suzaku-ōji, was to cleave the capital in half. Instead, the 300-foot-wide, willow-lined thoroughfare served only to segregate the prosperous eastern half of Heian-kyō from its undeveloped western counterpart. In time the disparity would grow so pronounced as to skew the layout of the city permanently to the right. Sakyō, the eastern sector, would spill across its natural boundary, the Kamo River, and mount the hills beyond. Ukyō, the neglected western sector, would languish for centuries, and in time rice fields would be planted between the broad parallel thoroughfares laid out by Chinese geomancers many decades before.

The flourishing eastern section of the capital contrived, at least for some time, to bear a superficial resemblance to the great residential areas of Ch'ang-an. Its streets were narrow, its houses inconspicuous, and its aura one of impermanence and anonymity. As has been previously observed, Heian-kyō would pay a high price for having chosen to emulate the T'ang. Wattle and thatch, shingles and sliding paper screens were the ingredients of impermanence — and also the fuel of flash fires. As a result, Heian-kyō was burned over so frequently that not a single structure from its early years has survived, and consequently the city's appearance, particularly in the first century of its existence, is largely a matter of conjecture.

According to the most authoritative sources, the mansions of ninth-century Heian-kyō were clustered

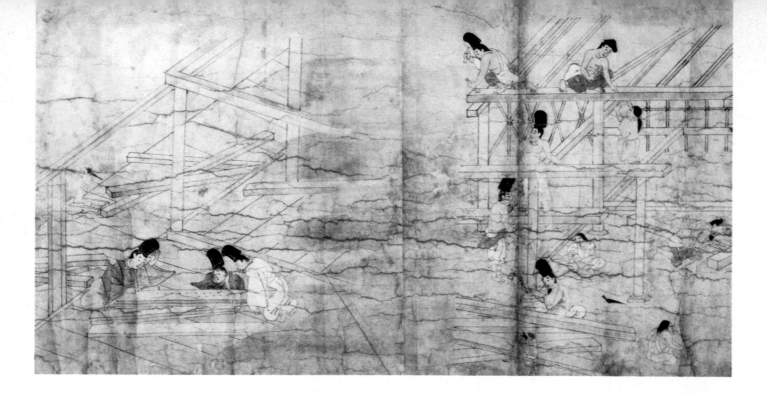

along the city's major avenues, generally within a mile of the imperial enclosure. These *shinden,* or private villas, were set in walled gardens that commonly covered three acres or more. Each lay secluded behind a high stone wall, and each was entered through an ornamental southern gate — both holdovers from the T'ang. Chinese tradition ended at the front gate, however; inside the residential compound the formality and opulence of the mainland model was abandoned in favor of a simple, rustic pavilion, situated toward the back of the lot and overlooking an often extensive garden. This garden itself was composed of traditional Chinese elements, artificial knolls and man-made ponds, but its role had altered perceptibly under Japanese influence. Through a process of transformation that was an altogether logical outgrowth of the Shinto belief in immanent godhead in all natural objects, the garden had in fact become the real heart of the residential compound. The residence itself was little more than an adjunct, whatever its size — an austere and unassuming shelter from the elements, constructed of such light native materials as unpainted cypress planking and plaited bamboo, materials that harmonized with, and visually reinforced, the naturalness of the setting.

Thus, almost from the outset, the great houses of Heian-kyō reflected the value that the Japanese placed upon simplicity and serviceability. These *shinden* have been labeled "the happiest products of Heian culture fusion," uniting as they did the classical elements of Chinese culture with a distinctive native informality and charm. As a result, the villas were often coveted by members of the imperial family, who preferred these cool retreats to the somewhat oppressive formality of the court. And as the practice of early abdication became increasingly frequent among Heian emperors, the need for a multiplicity of detached palaces grew correspondingly. In response to that need, Heian-kyō rapidly became a city of palaces, accommodating as many as five retired emperors and an untold number of pregnant imperial consorts. (Each of the latter was housed outside the imperial enclosure throughout her confinement, in accordance with ancient Shinto proscriptions against the defilement of the imperial residence.) The cost of these imperial building schemes was prodigious, and it was borne by an improvident government that could ill afford such luxuries. This state of affairs led one exasperated Fujiwara minister to declare, "At present the state is suffering from two things: building and warfare."

Improvisations upon the T'ang theme were not confined to private residences in the outer city; the imperial enclosure itself took on an emphatically Japanese appearance almost from the first. The Daidairi lay at the northern terminus of Suzaku-ōji — and here, too, obeisance to T'ang guidelines seemed to terminate at the gate. The inner city was an asymmetrical jumble of ceremonial halls, government offices, and private living quarters — largely lacking the studied separation of functions that characterized T'ang capitals. An attempt had clearly been made to apply the Chinese ideal to the layout of the Daidairi, but it was doomed by the complexity of the tasks that had to be performed within the imperial enclosure. In China, where civil ceremonial was distinct from religious observance, the physical separation of those activities was not only possible but preferable. In Heian-kyō, where those func-

Construction and conflagration were to recur in endless cycles during the first centuries of Kyoto's existence, and as a result carpenters such as those pictured at left were rarely without work. Their efforts were to little avail, however, for no sooner had a burned-over quarter of the city been restored than the fire demon (right) struck again.

tions were combined in the person of the emperor, integration was inevitable. In fact, it was to an important extent to determine the physical appearance of the imperial enclosure itself.

Immediately inside the enclosure's southern gate lay the Chōdō-in, a complex of stringently austere ceremonial halls. The perfect symmetry of the Chōdō-in was unique within the Daidairi, and logical in light of its function, which was to serve as a backdrop for the most formal and most solemn occasions of state. The broad central courtyard of the complex was ringed by twelve strikingly similar halls where, for thirty generations spanning some 370 years, ceremonies attending the coronation of Japan's emperors were performed. At the northern end of the Chōdō-in stood the Daigoku-den, the capital's principal hall of state. Its slim pillars were lacquered a bright red, its soaring roofs were covered with blue tiles, and dolphin-shaped finials capped its eaves. Inside, the imperial throne stood on a low dais at the center of the shallow reception hall, set off from the rest of the interior space by curtains hung in an octagon around it. According to Heian court chronicles, the Daigoku-den was inaugurated on New Year's Day in 796, some thirteen months after Kammu moved north from Nagaoka, and for centuries thereafter it was used for national celebrations, annual festivals, and the reception of foreign embassies.

On less formal occasions, the locus of imperial power shifted a few hundred yards northeast to the Kōkyo, official residence of the emperor himself. The double gate that admitted visitors to the imperial compound also served to signal a critical shift from Chinese ostentation to Japanese informality, further proof that the

Daidairi was a truly national institution. The first of these gates was a two-story structure whose red pillars and tiled roof reflected the dominant decorative motifs of the nearby Chōdō-in. The inner gate, on the other hand, was as Japanese as the outer was Chinese; it rose but a single story and was constructed entirely of traditional Japanese building materials. Beyond this gate lay the Shishin-den, the reception hall used by the emperor on all occasions that were not strictly governmental in nature. Its function corresponded to that of the Daigoku-den, but its appearance was distinctly less imposing. Its plank floors were unadorned, its approach a single wooden staircase.

Shortly after he took up residence in the Shishin-den, Kammu planted a plum tree near the southeast corner of the palace, and when that tree died some forty years later, Kammu's successor planted another in its stead. Court annals record that sometime thereafter the emperor "went to Shishin-den, and gave a banquet for his attendants." Then, "breaking off some flowers from the plum tree that stood by the building," he decorated the hair of the crown prince. Blight, age, and fire would kill a succession of these royal trees — first plum, then cherry — but the custom of replanting Kammu's tree became a firmly established imperial tradition, and except during periods of extreme national turmoil, a tree has always grown on the spot first selected by Kammu.

Having altered both the outward appearance and the original intent of so much of what they imported from China, the Japanese aristocracy of Kammu's day might reasonably have been expected to make fundamental changes in T'ang court ceremonial as well. That rigid

Although it was built a full millennium after its namesake, Kyoto's Old Imperial Palace (right) nonetheless preserves the essence of the original. This facsimile of Emperor Kammu's private quarters displays the same severity of line, absence of ornamental detail, and emphasis upon natural materials that characterized its predecessor. Moreover, it overlooks a flowering cherry tree that is descended — in spirit if not in fact — from the sapling that Kammu planted at the southeast corner of his palace in the first decade of the ninth century. Differing radically in appearance from the Heian Shrine, whose gardens are brightened each spring by an extraordinary display of irises (above), the Old Imperial Palace represents a major step in the evolution of a truly distinctive native architecture.

and minutely stratified system of class distinctions seemed, at least on the surface, antithetical to the demonstrated Japanese preference for ease and informality in their surroundings. Instead, the notion of noble rank — refined under the T'ang to a cap system whereby members of each aristocratic grade could be instantaneously identified by costume alone — was zealously adopted by the Japanese. In China, caps were supposedly awarded on the basis of merit; in Japan, where the notion of a meritocracy was widely mistrusted, the cap system served instead to reinforce the power of the hereditary aristocracy — a clear perversion of the system's original intent, but one with equally clear appeal to the powerful clan overlords assembled in Heian-kyō.

Not content merely to adopt the T'ang cap system, the Heian court stratified it still further. In 810, the court issued a series of proclamations governing the dress of all ten cap ranks and their numerous subdivisions, and eight years later prescribed modes of dress were assigned to the lower classes as well. At the same time, the crown released edicts regulating modes of behavior. This was the beginning of an increasingly labyrinthine system of sumptuary laws that were to lock the Heian court into a life-style that defied change for several centuries — and succumbed only when change finally succeeded in defying it.

With successive proclamations, this reductio ad absurdum was to acquire a force of its own, one that progressively involved the emperor in arbitrating matters of taste to the exclusion of more pressing matters of state. Thus deflected from his proper governance — often not altogether against his will — the emperor soon ceased to guide his realm in an effective political sense, a fact ambitious provincial overlords were quick to discern. In the years since their banishment from court, these provincial nobles had managed to extend their suzerainty over far wider areas than those first assigned to them. Peasants dwelling on adjacent lands had willingly ceded their holdings to these manor lords in exchange for protection from the crown and exemption from imperial taxes — and thus, throughout the tenth century, the tax base steadily dwindled. With the shifting of peasant allegiances, the corvée labor pool — so vital to major building projects in and around the capital — also shrank. Thousands of acres of border territory were brought under cultivation during this period, but the revenues from that acreage found their way into the coffers of provincial governors, not of the emperor. The collective impact of these developments was to siphon power away from the capital, encourage a new arrogance and independence among provincial governors, and ultimately bring the country full circle — back to the clan-focused society that had characterized prehistoric Japan.

Similarities between the *uji* system of fifth-century Japan and the complex prefeudal system of local governance in tenth-century Japan are only superficial, of course, for the impact of Chinese culture, the introduction of Buddhism, and the natural evolution of Japanese society had immensely complicated the political situation. For one thing, the phenomenal growth of Buddhism had forced every government since the Nara period to reach some accommodation with the bonzes who governed Japan's thriving Buddhist sects. This, too, was a part of Kammu's legacy, for it was he who had spurred the growth of two major Buddhist strong-

Supported by huge annual incomes derived from their provincial land holdings, the insular aristocrats of tenth-century Kyoto were free to indulge in totally frivolous leisure activities. Kemari, an informal and noncompetitive form of soccer, is the subject of the contemporary scroll painting at left. For those who preferred less strenuous forms of diversion there were cockfights (below), which regularly drew numbers of enthusiastic onlookers.

holds outside Heian-kyō, one on Mount Hiei, the other on Mount Kōya, southwest of the city. Indeed, the former had been founded in 805 by the priest Saichō at the specific request of the emperor himself. Hiei lay northeast of the new capital, in the quadrant known as the "Demon Quarter," the direction traditionally identified as the source of malign influences, and Kammu felt compelled to set up a mystical barricade on that flank. Saichō, who was chosen for the task, had recently returned from Mount T'ien-t'ai on the mainland, where he had been converted to the Lotus Sect of Buddhism. The tenets of his Tendai Sect, as the Japanese were to call it, had first distressed and then outraged the bonzes of Nara — and this had automatically given Saichō a natural ally in the emperor, whose antagonism toward the Nara monasteries was by then well established.

Saichō was the first of a long line of distinguished native ecclesiastics who, by infusing the Chinese model with a unique native sensibility, were to render Buddhism as distinctively Japanese as the Heian court hierarchy. Nowhere was this more evident than at Enrya-ku-ji, the monastery that he founded on Hiei. Chinese-style divination had inspired its settlement, and mystic Indian doctrines were preached from its temples, but Shinto *kami* inhabited its nether reaches, and their presence was not only acknowledged but welcomed by Saichō and his followers. Indeed, the founder of Enrya-ku-ji went so far as to openly venerate one of these gods as Sannō, King of the Mountain. From this time the worship of Shinto *kami* and Tendai bodhisattvas would become increasingly interrelated, and thus when, in 822, Tendai succeeded in establishing an ordination platform atop Hiei — in open defiance of Nara — the victory was one for Shinto as well as Tendai.

In 806 — a year after Saichō scaled Hiei — a fellow priest and close comrade named Kūkai returned to Heian-kyō from mainland China, bringing with him the teachings of the Shingon, or True Word, Sect. According to G. B. Sansom, the preeminent Western authority on early Japanese history, "Shingon — and to a lesser extent Tendai — is marked off from other Buddhist sects by its liking for magic and symbolism" — a fact that has much to do with the sect's popular acceptance by the lower classes. Both Tendai and Shingon were, coincidentally, less intellectual than the sects that preceded them, and the combination of greater accessibility and esoteric ritual appeal soon won the new monasteries scores of plebeian converts. Kūkai, who died in 816, is revered today not simply as the founder of modern Japan's largest and most flourishing Buddhist order, but also as the man who introduced tea to Japan. More importantly, Kūkai is credited with having invented or at least systematized the two syllabaries that made possible the first phonetic transcription of Japanese and hence the earliest native literature.

The remarkable secular success enjoyed by the major Heian Buddhist sects is attributable in part to the attitude of the Mahayana Buddhist teachings from which they were derived. Unlike Christianity in the West, Mahayana Buddhism was never to demand the exclusive allegiance of its adherents. Rather, it sought and won acceptance through its willing accommodation to preexisting native beliefs, even identifying native *kami* as manifestations of Buddhist deities. Shinto, for its part, remained a loose system of native beliefs, primi-

Emperor Kammu's geomancers identified the northeast quadrant of the compass as the "Demon Quarter" or "Devilgate." Evil spirits were said to lurk there, malign forces capable of scaling Mount Hiei and investing the capital itself. To prevent such an occurrence, Kammu sanctioned the establishment of the Buddhist monastery of Enryaku-ji atop Hiei. In time this magical barricade across the Devilgate would include some three thousand buildings, making it one of the largest temple complexes in the world. Only a few of those structures still stand, among them the rain-swept belltower seen below.

tive in its lack of a formal scripture, a church institution, and, indeed, a real theology. It therefore provided little resistance to the spread of the continental religion, and in point of fact it was only after Buddhism had become popular in Japan that the native system even acquired a name, *shintō* ("the way of the gods"), to distinguish it from *butsudō* ("the way of the Buddha").

It is clear that the initial rivalry that existed between the two religious groups was derived chiefly from conflicting political goals rather than from doctrinal differences. Buddhist institutions flourished most conspicuously under the powerful patronage of the Fujiwara, yet the imperial dynasty never abandoned its sacred priestly role, prescribed for all time by Shinto authority. Reconciled during the Heian period, the two faiths continued to exert considerable influence on the course of Japanese history into modern times.

With time the mountaintop retreats at Hiei and Kōya came to exercise temporal powers wholly inconsistent with the philosophies of their original founders. Enryaku-ji in particular became a lofty sanctuary for brigands and cutthroats, and in due course these criminals insinuated themselves into the monastery's hierarchy. A large standing army was formed, ostensibly to guard the complex against attacks from Nara but actually to further the ambitions of the renegade monks. Throughout the Heian period the bonzes of Hiei settled their quarrels with the crown by marching in force through the streets of Heian-kyō, bearing the sacred image of the god Sannō before them. Such confrontations rarely came to blows, for no member of the palace guard would risk damaging the revered image. On each occasion the emperor was compelled to acqui-

Twelve years after Kyoto was founded, a young priest named Kūkai returned from a brief sojourn in China to establish the Shingon Sect of Buddhism. Over the centuries this new sect was to become one of the largest and most popular in Japan, and its founder's reputation was to grow apace. Recognized in his own day as a master calligrapher and an accomplished sculptor, Kūkai is revered today as the inventor of the kana syllabary, the basis of written Japanese. Legend also credits Kūkai, the subject of the remarkably lifelike ninth-century wood carving at right, with the introduction of tea to Japan.

esce to this blatant spiritual blackmail, and on each occasion his capacity to govern effectively diminished fractionally for having done so.

Not illogically, the decline of the emperor's temporal power was to reveal certain weaknesses inherent in the cap system itself. Masked by the inflexibility of court protocol, which dictated an outward deference to the emperor that far exceeded his power to command, a bold usurpation of power occurred during the first half of the ninth century. The usurpers were the Fujiwara, a remarkable clan whose collective capacity for statecraft brought three centuries of serenity and progress to Heian-kyō — purchased, it was true, at an awesome price, but maintained nonetheless, long after the provincials had reverted to the more primitive ways of their forebears.

Initially, the relationship between the Fujiwara and the crown was a wholly symbiotic one: the former, acting as *sesshō,* or regent, during the minority of each new emperor, assured the integrity of the imperial line — guaranteeing the weakened crown against usurpers. Fujiwara no Yoshifusa, who was appointed *sesshō* to the nine-year-old emperor Seiwa in 866, half a century after the death of Kammu, was the first member of his family to hold the position — and the first *sesshō* who was not of royal birth. His son and successor, Motosune, served as regent to the boy-emperor Yōzei, who was deposed in 884 and replaced by the elderly and incompetent Kōkō. To ensure his continuing influence in the absence of an underage emperor, Motosune demanded that the position of *kampaku,* or regent to an adult emperor, be created. The crown was obliged to accede, and for the next 280 years a Fujiwara regent generally served as first chancellor — always acting through a reigning emperor, whose integrity he scrupulously observed. In fact, it was under the Fujiwara that the emperor was first accorded national adulation tantamount to public worship.

Fujiwara ascendancy dates from the mid-ninth century, but the family could trace its lineage back at least three centuries further, to Nakatomi no Kamatari, an architect of the Taika Reform. Kamatari, an ardent proponent of centralized government and strong monarchy, had been a formidable foe of the Soga, Buddhism's opportunistic early champions. Like the Soga, who created and deposed emperors at will during the early seventh century, the Fujiwara came to dominate and dictate the royal succession. They exercised that power in an entirely different manner, however. The Soga threatened; the Fujiwara cozened. The Soga assassinated ranking members of the imperial family; the Fujiwara married their daughters to future emperors. Indeed, this practice was the keystone of their policy, reviving the ancient concept of matrilineal descent for almost three centuries. In time, the genealogies of these two families became so intertwined that the Fujiwara were able to regulate the succession absolutely — and they saw to it that only the sons of Fujiwara consorts reached the throne.

To reinforce their control over the crown, successive Fujiwara *kampaku* encouraged emperors to abdicate after brief periods of rule, take holy orders, and retire to lavish villas outside the imperial enclosure. The prospect of a quiet, contemplative existence, free of the strictures of court life, undoubtedly held considerable appeal for many Heian emperors — and the few who

might have preferred to remain ensconced in the Kō-kyo would scarcely have dared to raise an objection. This pattern of early abdication, firmly established by the end of the ninth century, permitted the canny Fujiwara to deal with their rivals at court through a series of pliant, politically ignorant boy-emperors.

So skillful were the Fujiwara in their manipulation of the machinery of state that they were rarely, if ever, forced to resort to violence to achieve their aims. At the emperor's command — which is to say at his first chancellor's instigation — potential troublemakers were simply assigned to remote diplomatic outposts. They were rarely recalled. Consequently, Fujiwara authority remained absolute in Heian-kyō well into the twelfth century, long after the real political power in the country had shifted elsewhere. This remarkable endurance record must be attributed to Japan's clan system, which had always found its strength in the internal solidarity of the kinship group rather than in the merits of its particular members. This is not to suggest that the Fujiwara clan lacked distinguished and capable leaders. In truth, Japan has produced few national figures in its entire history to equal Fujiwara no Michinaga, whose tenure as de facto head of state lasted from 995 to 1028.

Michinaga never actually took the title of *kampaku*, as his father and two of his many brothers had, but then, he did not need to. As the uncle of two emperors, the grandfather of three more, and the chief minister to all, he could legitimately boast that he was "master of my world, like the flawless full moon riding the skies." Under Michinaga's able stewardship the fortunes of the Fujiwara rose to spectacular heights: their palaces rivaled the Kōkyo itself in splendor, and their combined income exceeded that of the imperial family.

Sometime around the year 1000, Michinaga ordered the construction of a small retreat on a site that had caught his eye near Uji, a village that lay southeast of the capital. The spot was undeniably lovely — worthy of far more imposing buildings — but the first chancellor was preoccupied with affairs of state throughout his career and consequently it remained for his son Yorimichi, last of the great Fujiwara ministers, to convert the villa into a magnificent temple. The resultant structure was Byōdō-in, the chief surviving monument and the enduring architectural glory of Heian-kyō's golden epoch. At one time the complex included a private temple, seven pagodas, and twenty-six smaller outbuildings. Of these, only the Phoenix Hall still stands, having survived where all else perished largely because it lay outside the city and was therefore spared the fires that regularly swept the metropolis. Vandals long ago stripped the lakeside pavilion of its inlaid ivory and gold, but they could not alter or erase the temple's essential lines, which are so delicate, so finely balanced, and so harmonious that they seem to carry the tiled roofs like weightless arcs upon the horizon.

All this munificence was purchased at a terrible price. By the end of the Fujiwara era, 80 per cent of the empire's revenue-producing land was held in *shōen*, the countryside had been ravaged by civil war, pirates infested the Inland Sea, bandits roamed the streets of the capital in broad daylight, and such law as prevailed outside the court itself was the law of individual clans. Minting of coins and compilation of official histories ceased, and land redistribution was abandoned entirely. The Fujiwara and their puppet sovereigns were at the mercy of any force that chose to lay siege to the capital — and yet, for scores of years, none did. In the calm eye of this political maelstrom the Fujiwara created a court culture of rare and exemplary beauty, so compelling and so enchanting that it marked the last century of the Heian period as the golden apex of Japanese civilization.

The outlines of ancient Heian-kyō have all but disappeared in the course of time, intervening centuries having worked their transformations upon the face of the Heian capital. Modern Kyoto reveals only faint traces of its earliest splendor, yet the city's Heian heritage remains at least partially accessible through a large body of writing — the first flowering of a unique vernacular literature. The culture to which this literary tradition belongs is that of the late Fujiwara period, the age when Heian-kyō achieved the promise of its ancient name: Capital of Peace and Tranquillity.

Two distinct, yet closely related, literary forms were to emerge almost simultaneously from Heian-kyō during the last decades of the tenth century. The first of these, the court diary, a derivative Chinese genre, is exemplified by Sei Shōnagon's epigrammatic, episodic, and highly idiosyncratic *Pillow Book*. The second of these forms, prose fiction, represented a truly radical departure from continental tradition, for the Chinese had long scorned such writing as trivial and second-rate. Murasaki Shikibu's *The Tale of Genji*, supreme manifestation of this new literary form, was not only the world's first novel, but also one of its longest and most complexly plotted. Significantly, both works were written in Japanese kana rather than Chinese characters, and both were written by women — perhaps be-

cause Heian courtiers, who prided themselves upon their imitative, formalized Chinese verse, dismissed kana as "women's writing."

The task of creating Japan's first true national literature thus fell to the women of the Heian court almost by default. Denied entrée into the rarefied world of Confucian scholarship, Lady Murasaki and her contemporaries chose to divert themselves by composing personal journals and random observations in their own tongue. *The Tale of Genji* would evolve out of these gossipy memoirs, which, taken together, provide an extraordinary record of daily life in tenth-century Heian-kyō — perhaps the most minutely detailed social chronicle ever produced.

The women of Fujiwara no Michinaga's time were well suited to their task, for they were treated with high esteem and extreme deference at court — at least in part because of the vital role they played in producing Fujiwara heirs to the throne. For the first time in Japanese history, girl babies were more prized than boy babies and women were accorded many of the legal privileges that men enjoyed. (Indeed, eight centuries were to elapse after the fall of the Fujiwara before women regained the respectability that they had enjoyed at the Heian court.) Thus encouraged to display the full range of their achievements, women turned with ease and eagerness to the composition of Heian's unofficial history.

Lady Murasaki's tale of Prince Genji, an exhaustive account of the amorous adventures of its eponymous hero, treated Heian's history in fictionalized form, but nonetheless with insight and candor. The result is a panoramic, detailed portrait of a culture dominated

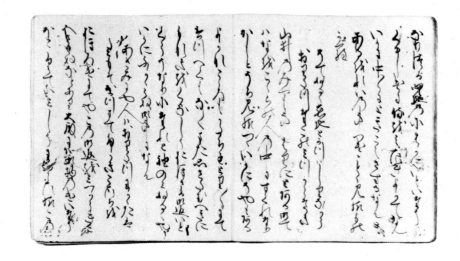

No work in all of Japanese fiction matches Lady Murasaki's The Tale of Genji *in fame, and few rival her epic in magnitude. Written around A.D. 1000 and illustrated roughly a century later, this exhaustively detailed chronicle of life at the imperial court has provided posterity with a remarkably faithful portrait of Kyoto's golden age. Of some eighty illustrations that once graced Lady Murasaki's text (right), only nineteen remain. These include the panel at left, which shows the sorrowing Prince Genji cradling the child born of his wife's liaison with another man.*

by aesthetic concerns — what G. B. Sansom called "the rule of taste." The overwhelming feature of the period was a highly refined sensitivity to beauty, a delicate sensibility that approached fastidiousness on the one hand and melancholia on the other. Style, not ethics, was the court's supreme concern, and by Murasaki's time beauty had all but eclipsed virtue as the true test of a person's worth. Consider, for example, this passage from *The Tale of Genji*:

> He was dressed in a suit of soft white silk, with a rough cloak carelessly slung over his shoulders, with belt and fastenings untied. In the light of the lamp against which he was leaning he looked so lovely that one might have wished he were a girl; and they thought that even Uma no Kami's "perfect woman," whom he had placed in a category of her own, would not be worthy of such a prince as Genji.

As Murasaki's description of Genji indicates, grooming and dress were vitally important to Heian aristocrats, who devoted hours to such mundane tasks as the selection of harmonizingly colored undergarments, as many as sixteen of which were worn at a time. Men shaved their temples, creating an artificially raised hairline, and women removed their eyebrows, painting false ones high on their foreheads. Both sexes wore heavy, dead-white makeup, and both were heavily perfumed, often with scents of their own devising.

Toilette and wardrobe were but the foundation of court life, however. Members of the aristocracy were also expected to write with an elegant hand — a man's calligraphic style being interpreted as a significant index to his character; a woman's, as a measure of her acceptability as a mistress. And they were expected to write often. Elaborate conventions were associated with letter writing, which played an important part in each stage of social interaction. No paramour worthy of the designation would begin his day without composing a "morning after" missive to his current amour, for instance. Such letters often contained brief poems, and poetry figured in daily conversation as well. It was said that a man's reputation could rise or fall on the composition of a single line of extemporaneous verse, and whereas that observation may be hyperbole, the implication is clear: the Heian court stressed the fine, rather than the martial, arts.

The nobles of Heian-kyō, freed of all but the most vacant sort of ceremonial obligations and sustained by revenues from *shōen* they rarely visited, lived from festival to festival. To distract themselves in the intervening hours they visited temples, practiced calligraphy, exchanged poetry, and gossiped passionately. Dalliances were proposed, letters composed, assignations arranged, trysts kept, affairs consummated, and liaisons broken off in endless cycles. Promiscuity was the norm, chivalry unheard of, and responsibility virtually nonexistent. Indolent, self-indulged, parochial, and politically powerless, the aristocratic minority that dwelled within the walls of Heian-kyō lived an aimless and ambivalent existence. They took no interest in affairs of state or the plight of the lower classes — which, as Genji himself observed, "do not concern us." They represented less than one-tenth of one per cent of the nation's population, yet they annually disposed of a wildly disproportionate share of its income. Small wonder then that the nobles of the Heian court were known, even in their own time, as "dwellers among the clouds."

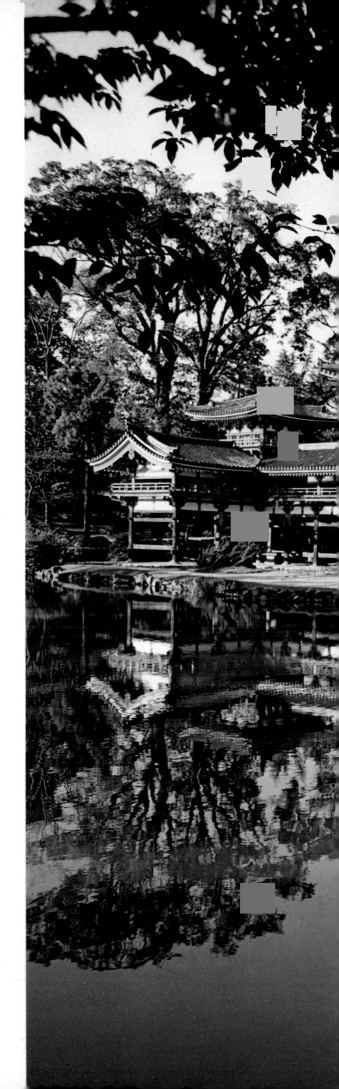

By the beginning of the eleventh century, the illustrious
Fujiwara clan had managed to consolidate their position
as the effective masters of the Japanese state. Family
members filled virtually every important ministerial post,
and the clan's preeminent statesman, Fujiwara no
Michinaga, actually set policy for the crown. It was
Michinaga who ordered the construction of a small family
villa at Uji, southeast of Kyoto, but it was his son and heir
Yorimichi who converted that site into the splendid
temple complex of Byōdō-in. Thirty-four buildings once
stood near the reflecting pond at Byōdō-in, but only
one survives — the renowned Phoenix Hall (right). True
to its avian name, this feather-light structure appears to
float above the water, suspended on wings of painted
wood. It is without question the supreme architectural
achievement of the Fujiwara age — and it houses that
era's greatest work of art, an eleven-foot-high seated
Buddha (above) attributed to the sculptor Jōchō.

III

The Way of the Warrior

The middle decades of the eleventh century provided a critical test of the resiliency of the Japanese monarchy — and, by extension, of the entire concept of the imperial household's semidivine status. If ever the emperor and his cloud-dwelling retinue stood in peril of coercion or conquest — or even outright extinction — it was in the years immediately following the death of Fujiwara no Yorimichi, the last of his clan's great statesmen. By that time, the warrior-monks of Mount Hiei, who had grown more brazen with each unchallenged foray into the capital, had demoralized the populace and paralyzed the aristocracy. During the regency of Yorimichi, the bonzes of Enryaku-ji had dared to march, three thousand strong, upon the palace of the chancellor himself, and a few years later two rival monasteries had assembled some 40,000 troops in the very heart of Heian-kyō. At this same time, street brawling between the great clans — led by the Taira and the Minamoto — was to become commonplace.

The crown was powerless to repel these raids, and the royal purse — used over the preceding century to buy armed protection from Taira and Minamoto alike — was all but empty. Yet despite the instability of the government, a proliferation of emperors, retired emperors, regents, and retainers continued to maintain the pretense of rule in the capital. The crown's most loyal servants, the Fujiwara, clung to the last vestiges of their once-considerable power by playing their less experienced opponents against one another. For a time, prestige alone held this frail fabric together, for even the crudest provincial barons recognized the emperor's person as sacrosanct and acknowledged his line to be the single unbroken thread linking eleventh-century Japan

to its glorious past. To snap that thread would have been unthinkable; the royal line was at all costs to be maintained. This inviolable national obligation served to shield the Fujiwara as well as the throne, and it was not until the clan had been weakened by internal dissent that its enemies dared to rise against it.

The first major rift in the Fujiwara clan's solidarity had come in the 930's, when a chieftain named Sumitomo broke with his regent and the crown and established a loose dominion over western Japan. Sumitomo was captured and executed in 941, but by that time the Fujiwara ministers had been forced to contend with a second large-scale rebellion, this one in the east, where a Taira chieftain had laid claim to eight provinces in the Kantō region and boldly styled himself "the new emperor."

To suppress these rebellions — and simultaneously to sweep the Inland Sea of pirates — the court had enlisted the aid of the Minamoto clan, whose continued service to the regency was to earn them the nickname "claws and teeth of the Fujiwara." A pattern was thus established whereby the Fujiwara bartered imperial favors — in the form of provincial posts and tax-exempt estates — in exchange for protection from their increasingly powerful rivals. The clan's capacity to do so was fixed, of course, for Japan had a limited amount of arable acreage, and by the end of their tenure the Fujiwara *kampaku* had ceded four-fifths of the nation's taxable lands in exchange for a few years of grace.

The risings that broke out in the 930's were largely attributable to negligence on the part of the Fujiwara, and both rebellions were rather easily suppressed when the threat they posed was finally perceived at court. To

prevent the occurrence of similar episodes in the future, the Fujiwara undertook to seed the countryside — particularly Taira strongholds — with supposedly loyal members of contending clans, chief among them the Minamoto. This shrewd attempt to balance — and therefore undermine — provincial authority was effective at first, but fatally expensive in the long run, for the Minamoto demanded immunity from taxation in exchange for their watchdog services in the hinterlands, thus accelerating the growth of vast provincial *shōen*.

Ironically enough, the first major outside assault upon the prestige of the Fujiwara was launched from above, not from below. In 1068, in a bold reassertion of imperial authority, Emperor Go-Sanjo freed the crown of Fujiwara dominance. To do so, he capitalized on developments that had been building for a number of years, among them the failure of Fujiwara women to produce sufficient female offspring to ensure a constant comingling of Fujiwara and royal blood. By mid-century the kinship tie was no longer absolute, and by 1068 the clan was sufficiently weakened that it could not block the accession of Go-Sanjo, who was neither the son nor the husband of a Fujiwara lady. Moreover, the new emperor was not a child but an independent adult who ruled without consulting his *kampaku*.

After a reign of only four years, Go-Sanjo relinquished his throne to Shirakawa, another brilliant and dynamic exception to the rule that Late Heian monarchs were blandly apolitical and largely occupied with the petty affairs of the court. Shirakawa ruled for fourteen years before abdicating, and his retirement proved every bit as remarkable as his rule had been. Although ensconced in a luxurious retirement villa and attired in the robes of a Buddhist priest, Shirakawa continued to function as the *éminence grise* in Heian politics. This curious development, known as *insei* or "cloister government," was to persist for half a century and end only with the rise of the Taira clan and the final dissolution of the Fujiwara regency. During this period, Japan was ruled by a succession of retired emperors who controlled the complex machinery of state through subservient Fujiwara ministers — to whom the reigning emperor was, in turn, obedient. This elaborate double-blind system of government could scarcely cope with problems of local administration, let alone national crises, and its collapse waited only the rise of a truly paramount provincial clan.

No single clan had gained supremacy by the year 1100, but the ceaseless contention among them had dramatically reshaped Japanese society. As conditions in the provinces deteriorated, the cloister government in Heian-kyō had been forced to deputize increasing numbers of provincial governors to act as regional military police — creating, in essence, small standing armies in virtually every corner of the realm. At this same time, the managers of the great outlying *shōen* had been compelled to take up arms to defend their holdings, and during the late eleventh century these groups had begun to coalesce into *bushidan,* local mutual protection societies modeled upon traditional kinship patterns. The rise of a provincial military aristocracy, whose members were known either as *bushi* or *samurai,* was the dominant feature of the age — a return, in one sense, to the lord-vassal relationships of the Yamato era.

The massive realignment of class loyalties that occurred during this period was a predictable outgrowth

The epic clash between the Taira and Minamoto clans, twelfth-century Japan's greatest feudal powers, was to span almost thirty years. The Minamoto were the ultimate victors in this protracted civil conflict, but the first major battle test — which came in 1160 — resulted in a Taira triumph. Shortly thereafter a band of Minamoto rebels forced their way into Kyoto and seized Emperor Nijō, whom they held prisoner in the imperial palace. The emperor's subsequent escape and flight to the Taira stronghold of Rokuhara is the subject of a famous contemporary scroll. In the detail shown below, Emperor Nijō — disguised as a woman — is assisted into an ox-drawn cart at the outset of his journey to Rokuhara.

of the decline of the centralized state, for as British historian G. B. Sansom has noted, except in Heian-kyō itself this was an age when "land mattered more than honours, and force was more effective than law." It comes as no surprise, then, that the peasants of Late Heian Japan allied themselves with the prominent landholders, who secured their huge estates by force of arms, rather than with the effete, ineffectual, and impoverished court of distant Heian-kyō. When rebellion broke out in the north in 1051, its suppression was, in a sense, a triumph of force over law, for although the victory was claimed by the crown, the agent of that victory was one of these local lords. It was Minamoto no Yoriyoshi who annihilated that rebel army, not some Fujiwara commander. And Yoriyoshi was a follower of Hachiman, the Shinto god of war. The Minamoto triumph was Hachiman's triumph as well, and it marked the emergence of a distinct military caste in Japanese society, one with its own traditions and its own moral and legal codes.

The final blow to the tottering Fujiwara regency came in 1156 and was mounted by Kiyomori, leader of the Taira faction. In characteristically Japanese fashion, Kiyomori disguised his bid for power as a gesture of support for Emperor Go-Shirakawa, who was determined to strip the ex-emperor Sutoku of his *insei* powers. For the first time in Japanese history, court factions were to resort to military action to resolve their differences, and the appalled citizens of Heian-kyō were treated to the spectacle of Taira and Minamoto armies dueling in the streets of the unfortified, ungarrisoned capital. The Hogen Insurrection, as that conflict was known, ended with a decisive victory for Go-Shira-

kawa's troops. The vanquished Minamoto, who had sided with Sutoku and the Fujiwara, retreated to their provincial strongholds, and their power at court quickly evaporated. From this time on, the Taira would dominate the home provinces while the Minamoto exercised control over parts of the Kantō.

Peace had scarcely been restored to the capital when, in 1160, the great Minamoto chieftain Yoshitomo foolishly joined a conspiracy to overthrow Taira no Kiyomori. Taking advantage of the Taira leader's temporary absence from the city, the rebels seized both the emperor and his cloistered predecessor. The conspirators were no match for the Taira in cunning, however, and the latter promptly engineered the escape of the ex-emperor. A short time later the emperor, disguised as a lady-in-waiting, slipped away from his captors and made his way to the Taira headquarters. Their combined forces then turned upon the rebels, who were holed up in the imperial palace itself, and the would-be usurpers were forced to flee ignominiously from Heian-kyō. Once again victory belonged to the Taira, and this time their vengeance was particularly terrible: they slaughtered every Minamoto warrior they could lay their hands upon, sparing only the boy Yoritomo and his younger half brother Yoshitsune.

With his Fujiwara rivals vanquished and the Minamoto line all but expunged, Kiyomori was supreme at court, and he wasted little time in insinuating himself and his family into the offices once held by the Fujiwara. Over the next two decades, he succeeded in placing sixteen close relatives in high court posts while elevating thirty-six others to somewhat lower ranks. By 1180, Kiyomori, who had technically retired as prime minister, had even succeeded in placing his grandson Antoku on the throne. This pattern of crude imitation of Fujiwara policy with regard to the court hierarchy and the succession earned Kiyomori few friends at court, and in May of that year Minamoto no Yorimasa led his clansmen, dissident priests, and members of the imperial family against the durable Taira overlord. Although the abortive coup was ruthlessly extinguished, the flame of rebellion it had kindled could not be put out. In the Minamoto-held Izu Peninsula the survivors began to gather under the banner of Yoritomo, who had grown to manhood in the years since the bloodletting of 1160.

To the citizens of the strife-torn capital, the middle decades of the twelfth century must have seemed black indeed. The city's streets had become a battlefield, with contending armies assaulting one another with casual disregard for the horrified populace of the Capital of Peace and Tranquillity. The 1180 rising was no exception, and it was not until Yorimasa's forces had been decisively beaten that the conflict's epicenter shifted away from the capital. With the Taira close on his heels, Yorimasa fled south toward Nara, pausing en route to burn the bridge at Uji. Undeterred, Kiyomori's troops plunged into the water, forded the stream, and forced Yorimasa to make a final stand at Byōdō-in. The outcome of the battle was never really in question, and as the Taira closed in on Yorimasa's decimated band, the proud Minamoto general quietly committed suicide in front of the Phoenix Hall.

The events of March 1180 so unnerved Kiyomori that the crusty dictator actually abandoned Heian-kyō several months later, resettling in his family's provin-

The climactic battle of the Gempei War, the sea duel at Dan-no-ura, resulted in the annihilation of the last remnants of the once-mighty Taira army. Only a handful of noncombatants were spared, among them the Taira emperor's mother, Kenreimon-in, who was carried to Kyoto by the victorious Minamoto. The sorrowing ex-empress spent the rest of her days in pious seclusion at Jakkō-in (left), a tiny nunnery northeast of the capital.
Overleaf:
In the long course of the Taira-Minamoto conflict, fighting frequently erupted in the streets of Kyoto itself. This panel from a famed thirteenth-century scroll painting, records the destruction by fire of the imperial palace during an early phase of the protracted contest.

cial seat of Fukuhara. The Taira leader soon discovered that it was impossible to exercise effective control over the government from this outpost, however, and six months later he abandoned Fukuhara and moved the entire court back to Heian-kyō. Kiyomori himself died shortly thereafter, but the Taira-Minamoto conflict, now known as the Gempei War, raged on for four more years. By 1183 the Taira were clearly on the defensive. Yoritomo was undisputed master of the Kantō, and the focus of the war had shifted permanently westward to the Yamato. The Taira spent 1184 retreating down the Inland Sea, island by island, but the following year they were finally cornered at Dan-no-ura, where the last remnants of their once-mighty army were summarily dispatched in a great sea battle. The carnage was awesome: it all but eliminated the Taira line, and in the process it gave rise to a local legend that the strange markings on the crabs of Dan-no-ura Bay are the faces of Taira ghosts.

When the battle at Dan-no-ura turned against the Taira, Kiyomori's widow, who had fled south with the remains of her husband's army, leaped into the sea with the boy-emperor Antoku in her arms — and the rest of the emperor's retinue followed suit. Antoku's mother, Empress Kenreimon-in, fully intended to join the hapless Taira in their watery grave, but alert Minamoto sailors pulled her from the sea by her hair and returned her to Heian-kyō, where she ultimately entered the tiny nunnery of Jakkō-in. There a ten-foot-square cell, divided into an oratory and a bedchamber, was constructed for the grieving ex-empress, whose renunciation of imperial luxury was complete and unwavering.

News of Kenreimon-in's altered circumstances even-

tually reached ex-emperor Go-Shirakawa, who decided to pay her an unannounced visit. Setting out from his palace — ostensibly incognito — in the company of a score of courtiers and guards, the emperor made his way up the narrow valley in which Jakkō-in was situated, ascending at last the steep, deeply shaded steps that brought visitors to the nunnery itself. The ensuing encounter between the magnificently robed sovereign and the humbly clad nun was painful for them both. As the afternoon progressed and Kenreimon-in retailed her unhappy story, Go-Shirakawa was moved to tears. He returned to his palace shaken and somewhat chastened, and immediately sat down to compose a bittersweet verse recollection of his experience.

The epic conflict between the Taira and Minamoto, like that of their Florentine contemporaries the Guelphs and the Ghibellines, is replete with semilegendary tales. Indeed, the period of the Gempei War is often identified as the most colorful chapter in all of Japanese history, one which gave rise to a new literature that glorified not only the great clan leaders but the new warrior class as a whole. The notion of heavily armed aristocrats meeting one another in single combat was as appealing in the East as in the West, and such encounters, in almost endless permutation, were the basis of Japan's first popular literature, the chivalrous romances of the Gempei War.

It is doubtful whether any of the thousands of tales generated by the clash of the great clans is as well-known as the tragic story of Yoshitsune, Yoritomo's younger brother, who is said to have spent his childhood in exile in Kurama, north of Kyoto. According to the *Gikeiki,* the most popular version of the romance

of Yoshitsune, the young Minamoto outcast was taught fencing and the other martial arts by *tengu,* the long-nosed goblins that inhabit the dark forests of Kurama. He was soon given an opportunity to put these skills to the test, for while crossing the Gojō Bridge in Kyoto he was set upon by Benkei, whom the *Gikeiki* describes as "a great, bold, brawling monk, ingenious, irrepressible, and irreverent, who is nevertheless sensitive, patient, subtle, learned, and accomplished." Yoshitsune, who was still in his teens at the time of this encounter, easily bested the cocksure Benkei, and the two thereafter became inseparable comrades-in-arms.

It was Yoshitsune who led the Minamoto forces to victory over the Taira at Dan-no-ura in 1185, but that personal triumph served only to irritate the envious Yoritomo, who refused to receive his brother when the latter returned from battle. For three weeks Yoshitsune lingered outside his older brother's camp. "Though innocent, I am blamed; though deserving, and guilty of no error, I have incurred His Lordship's displeasure," Yoshitsune wrote. "What can I do but weep bitter tears?" he added. "I have been denied the privilege of seeing His Lordship for so long that the blood bond between us seems to have vanished." His appeal, which fell upon deaf ears, contained an evocation of the warrior's life that seemed to many to capture the very essence of the samurai ideal:

> So that I might demolish the Taira men, I whipped my mount over precipitous cliffs, heedless of life in the face of the enemy; I braved the perils of wind and wave on the boundless sea, ready to sink to the bottom as food for monsters of the deep. Battle dress was my pillow; arms were my profession. . . .

Rebuffed and embittered, Yoshitsune withdrew to the countryside, and there began assembling troops against his brother. Yoritomo, alerted to the incipient coup, launched a ferocious counterattack — and Yoshitsune and Benkei were forced to flee northward to take refuge with a provincial chieftain. Little more than two years later the harried warriors' protectors turned upon them, and Yoshitsune and his intrepid band were obliged to take their own lives to avoid capture.

Outcast, adventurer, field commander, would-be usurper, and fugitive — Yoshitsune had been all of these in just three decades. His life of privation and service, his casual contempt for death and equal disregard for material possessions, and, finally, his choice of suicide over the shame of capture — all made him an enormously sympathetic model of samurai virtues. Indeed, he seemed the embodiment of the unwritten code of *bushidō,* "the way of the warrior," which dictated total fealty, selfless service, constant vigilance, and death before dishonor. (Adherence to the last of these dictates was, in time, to become so zealous that the form of ritual suicide known as *seppuku* — or, more vulgarly, *harakiri,* "belly slashing" — came to obscure other equally significant aspects of *bushidō.*) The symbols of the samurai were the sword and the cherry blossom, and in Japanese eyes, at least, the one was every bit as important as the other. The great two-handed sword was the warrior's chief weapon, an awesomely sharp laminated blade that could easily part a human body at the waist — through a full suit of armor.

The cherry blossom was an abstraction, its evanescent beauty a reminder of the transience of all life, especially that of a warrior pledged to die in service to his master. But it was more than that, as Yukio Mishima, the twentieth-century novelist who emulated the samurai in life and imitated them in death, has observed. "To combine action and art is to combine the flower that wilts and the flower that lasts forever," Mishima has written, suggesting that the lone warrior, the man of action, is indeed foredoomed, but that the warrior's martial arts and moral code endure. The blossom also suggested an entirely different dimension of these supposedly unrefined fighting men. That other facet was the samurai's appreciation of the elemental beauty of nature, a quality that was truer to the Shinto spirit of Yamato Japan than to the Sinicized artificiality of Heian-kyō.

An appreciation of the cardinal samurai virtues — simplicity, directness, and a sentimental respect for indigenous institutions — explains why the warrior class no less than the masses readily adopted the simple Buddhist doctrines that achieved new prominence in the late twelfth century. The first of these doctrines to receive widespread attention was Jōdo, or Pure Land, which was formalized by the Tendai monk Hōnen Shōnen after 1175. It was Hōnen's contention that salvation lay in the repeated chanting of Amida Buddha's name, not in the recondite doctrines of the great monasteries. In a time of civil turmoil and general public apprehension, the appeal of Hōnen's uncomplicated pathway to salvation was enormous. The foreboding "latter days of the law," long prophesied by the Buddhist sages, seemed to be at hand, and the masses gravitated readily, even zealously, toward the promise of a serene hereafter. For the first time since its introduction, Buddhism had been made fully accessible to the masses — and when Hōnen's pupil Shinran simplified the master's doctrine, conversions became legion.

With the introduction of the Nichiren Sect some decades later, the evolution of a distinctively Japanese form of Buddhism reached its final, critical stage. Nichiren, the founder of the sect, was unlike any of his famous predecessors in that he was both militant and nationalistic. "I will be the eyes of Japan," he vowed. "I will be the great vessel of Japan." Nichiren's messianic determination to save his country from what he saw to be its internal corruption led him to break the tacit covenant of toleration that had been a distinctive feature of Japan's religious history for centuries. Nichiren preached that all other sects were heretical, but he saved his most vitriolic invective for the newest Buddhist order, Zen, which he labeled "a doctrine of fiends and devils."

Outwardly, Nichiren's sect would seem to have had little to fear from the adherents of Zen, a group that scarcely proselytized. But the overzealous monk's apprehension was in fact well-grounded, for Zen was to prove the most important of all the doctrines imported from the mainland. It would never attract the following that the Pure Land and the Nichiren sects had, but its peculiar, enigmatic doctrine would profoundly reshape Japanese ethics, aesthetics, art, and architecture.

On first inspection, Zen hardly qualified as a religion, let alone as a threat to the well-established Nichiren Sect. Zen, a name derived from the Sanskrit word for meditation, differed markedly from the other Buddhist sects in emphasizing that enlightenment came solely through direct intuitive perception. It eschewed formal scriptures in favor of *kōan,* the baffling epi-

grams that Westerners find amusing, provocative, and disturbing. And it stressed self-reliance, extreme austerity, and rigorous self-discipline bordering on asceticism — values that paralleled, on a religious plane, the social and moral strictures of *bushidō,* thereby assuring the sect's acceptance by the samurai class.

Zen had actually been known in Japan since the time Heian-kyō was founded, but not until the thirteenth century did a resurgence of contact with China spur two Tendai priests, Eisai and his highborn disciple Dōgen, to establish fledgling Zen sects in the capital. Eisai founded Kyoto's first Zen monastery, Kennin-ji, during the early years of the century, and Dōgen, who modified Zen to conform with the temperament of the samurai class, introduced the concept of *zazen,* or sitting in meditation, to Japan.

Zen flourished as the thirteenth century progressed, and both Kyoto and Kamakura soon boasted impressive Zen Sect temple complexes. The most important were ranked as the *Gosan,* the Five Monasteries, and the greatest of these was Daitoku-ji, founded in 1325 in Murasakino, the "Purple Plain" that lay along Kyoto's northern periphery. The vermilion gates and looming, shedlike halls of this complex are attributed to Akamatsu Norimura, a priest summoned to the capital around 1309 by the future emperor Go-Daigo, who had taken a keen interest in the new sect. The Chinese-style temple that rose under Akamatsu's supervision so caught Go-Daigo's fancy that in 1334 he penned an official declaration — still in the temple's possession — to the effect that Daitoku-ji was the Zen temple *par excellence* of the court.

Not surprisingly, Zen encountered early opposition

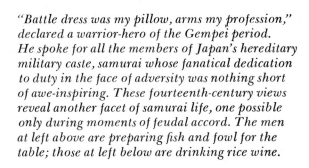

from the popular Buddhist sects, for it stressed personal enlightenment rather than dependence upon Amida Buddha's boundless grace. It endured, in the face of such powerful opposition, at least in part because it had found powerful patrons in the Minamoto, whose victory at Dan-no-ura had catapulted them to a position of supreme political power. Yoritomo, the architect of that victorious campaign, had seen only too clearly the folly of attempting to replicate the Fujiwara regency, imitated by the Taira during their brief ascendancy. Wanting nothing to do with Kyoto and its aristocratic conceits, Yoritomo had settled in Kamakura, a small coastal village where the Minamoto had long maintained a shrine to Hachiman. There he established Japan's first comprehensive feudal government, the Kamakura shogunate, which was to be the template for a succession of military regimes destined to dominate the nation until the imperial restoration of 1868.

The Kamakura government was not content to leave feudal practice undefined, and it soon developed its own legal codes and institutions based upon Minamoto house law. The new government was vastly more effective than the system it superseded, permitting the shogun to rule the entire nation through a taut network of alliances. On one level, Kamakura functioned as the military headquarters of the Minamoto vassal group, a firm system of subordination that had grown to include more than two thousand separate military bands seeded throughout the provinces. On another level, Kamakura served as the center of the nation's civil administration. There highly efficient bureaucrats — some of them imported from Kyoto — impartially dispensed justice, collected taxes, and settled disputes with the backing of

The great temples of Nara, extensively damaged in the first few years of the Gempei War, were rebuilt during the Minamoto period. The restoration of Kōfuku-ji, whose numerous treasures include the guardian statue below, sparked a sculptural renaissance in twelfth-century Japan. Inspired by the artistic ideals of the Nara period — which had produced such striking statues as the life-size clay figure opposite — Kyoto sculptors created robustly realistic works to glorify the new shogunate. Sanjūsangendō, Kyoto's Hall of Thirty-three Bays (right), boasts the paramount examples of their splendid work.

the shogunate. In Kyoto, some three hundred miles to the west, a special lord protector and his garrison kept a watchful eye on the restive imperial court.

One of the new government's first official acts was to assist in the restoration of Kōfuku-ji and Tōdai-ji, the great Nara monasteries that had been razed during the first phase of the Gempei War. Rampaging Taira troops had also mutilated the Great Buddha of Tōdai-ji, and the repair of that bronze colossus sparked the sculptural renaissance for which the Kamakura period is justly celebrated. The sculptors who were brought south from the capital in 1183 to undertake those repairs were descendants of Jōchō, creator of the magnificent statue of the Amida Buddha that dominates the interior of the Phoenix Hall at Byōdō-in, and they were as talented as their fabled predecessor. They executed their commission with skill and sensitivity, but saved their best efforts for the greatest expression of Kamakura art, the Sanjūsangendō, or Hall of Thirty-three Bays, in the capital. The somber exterior of Sanjūsangendō belies the splendor that lies within, where gilded Kannons — 1,001 of them — range the length of the hall, whose center is occupied by a great Kannon with eleven faces and a thousand arms.

The restoration of Nara and the cultivation of a new and more naturalistic art were calculated gestures on the part of Yoritomo, gestures designed to win the allegiance of the people while establishing an artistic identity for the Kamakura shogunate that was both individual and appealing. In recognizing the efficacy of such a policy, as in so many other respects, Yoritomo was a man of unusual energy and vision. His blind spot was the succession, which he entrusted to two ineffectu-

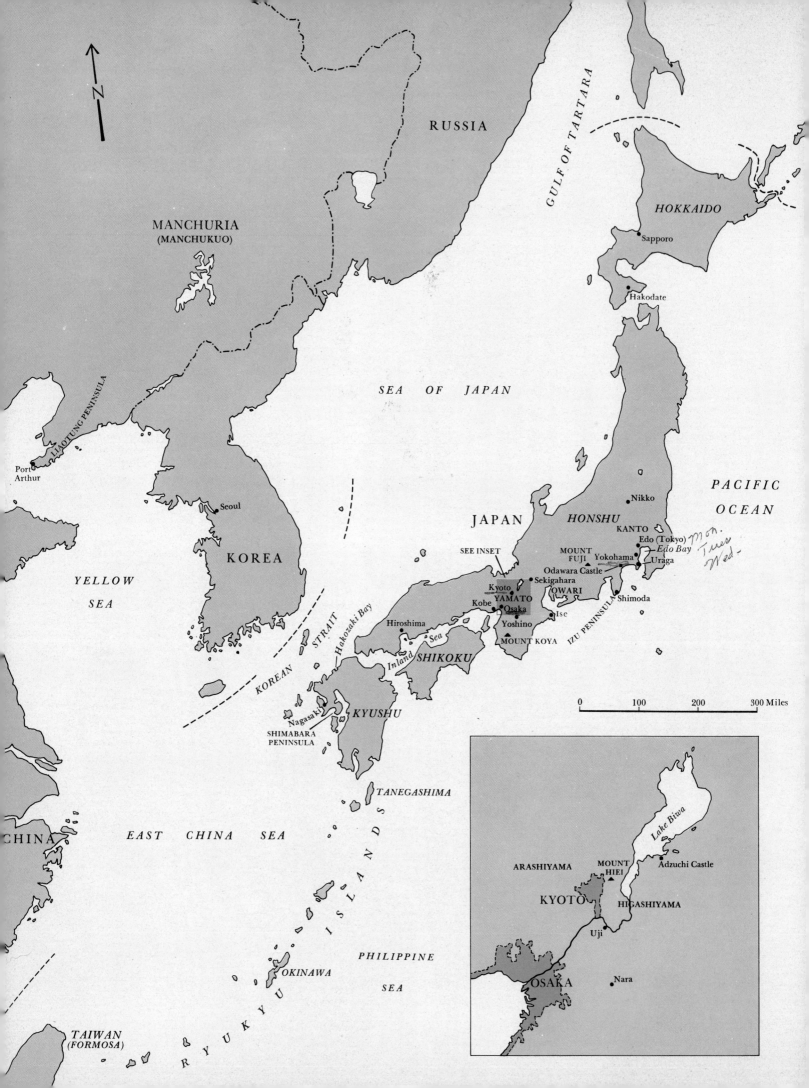

al sons. After Yoritomo's death the government fell into disarray, and only the intriguing of the shogun's widow prevented a swift coup. To maintain hold on the shogunate, Yoritomo's widow had her father, Hōjō Tokimasa, appointed regent to her sons. For the next hundred years, Hōjō regents exercised the same sort of control over the shogunate in Kamakura that the Fujiwara had once exercised over the emperor in Kyoto. Thus, for a time, Japan was governed at three removes: the emperor was but a spokesman for the cloistered ex-emperor, who was answerable to the shogun, who was a puppet of the Hōjō regent.

In 1221 the ex-emperor Go-Toba, seeking to subvert this cumbrous machinery, covertly raised an army of his own in the capital. Alerted to Go-Toba's ambitions, the Hōjō regents reacted quickly. In less than two months the rising had been quashed, the emperor and his followers banished, and numerous aristocrats executed. The Kamakura government needed no more substantial excuse to appropriate the *shōen* of the capital's wealthiest families, and the shogunate's subsequent campaign against the landed aristocracy permanently reduced the strength of the imperial court.

By mid-century, a host of unforeseen calamities had conjoined to plague the efficient bureaucracy in Kamakura. In 1257, a particularly severe earthquake had rocked the entire district, followed two years later by an outbreak of plague in the city itself. Bad as matters were, they would presently grow worse, for a far more deadly menace was shortly to invade Japan. In 1263, Kublai Khan succeeded in uniting all of North China under his Mongol banner, and five years later turned his attention to Japan, whose emperor he identified in his official communiqué as "the ruler of a small country." His letter demanding tribute contained an invasion threat that reduced the court to near hysteria, but the shogunate remained steadfast. Kublai's envoys were rebuked, and successive Chinese embassies returned to the mainland empty-handed, the last in 1273.

Less than a year later, an army of 26,000 men set sail from Korea in some 900 troop convoys built by China's Korean vassals and manned by 6,700 Korean seamen. The invasion fleet—the first the Japanese had ever faced—landed on Kyushu two weeks later. Local samurai bands, distinctly outnumbered and frankly terrified of the explosive devices the Mongols were using, nonetheless attacked immediately, without waiting for reinforcements from Kamakura. The Mongols, disconcerted by the ferocity of the resistance they encountered, withdrew. That night a powerful gale struck the invasion fleet as it rode at anchor. The armada stood out to sea, but before it could reach safety the fleet was decimated and some 13,500 men were lost.

Undaunted by the expense and the inconclusiveness of this initial encounter, the Great Khan sent another embassy to Japan, this time demanding that the ruler himself journey to Peking to do obeisance at the Chinese court. The infuriated regent responded by slaying the Chinese envoys and exhibiting their heads on pikes throughout the city—a gesture certain to incur the Great Khan's legendary wrath. So convinced were the Japanese that a second invasion would be forthcoming that the entire nation began to gird for it. The men of Kyushu built a series of fortifications around Hakozaki Bay, whose sheltered beaches had already served one Mongol force and might well tempt

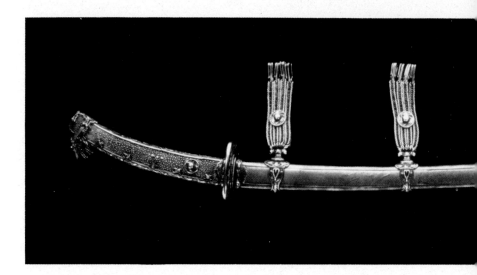

another. A fleet of small, highly maneuverable warships was built, and crews were trained to handle them. A census was taken in Kyushu, and an official roll of all those deemed capable of bearing arms was compiled. Weapons were stockpiled, and the entire nation went on a round-the-clock war alert.

At this stage the Japanese received a desperately needed respite of almost five years, during which Kublai was preoccupied with subduing the Southern Sung dynasty. Finally, in June of 1281, the long-anticipated invasion began. The attack came in two waves, with 40,000 Mongols and Koreans crossing the strait at roughly the same time that 100,000 more soldiers were embarking from southern China. The first contingent landed near Hakozaki on June 23, and was eventually augmented by other squadrons. The ensuing struggle, which lasted almost two months, proved inconclusive; the Mongols were unable to penetrate inland, and the Japanese could not drive them back into the sea. Then, on the fiftieth day of the invasion attempt, a great wind rose and for forty-eight hours Kyushu was ripped and battered by a dreadful typhoon. The storm itself was seasonal and consequently not altogether unexpected, but its timing was so providential that the Japanese named it a *kamikaze,* or "divine wind." (In much the same manner Elizabethan England, some three centuries later, would speak of the "Protestant wind" that scattered the Spanish Armada.) Of the 4,400 ships outfitted for the expedition, only two hundred are said to have returned to China; and of the invading army of 140,000, fewer than 30,000 survived.

The Kamakura shogunate had met the severest test in the nation's history and apparently survived. Ap-

pearances were deceiving, however, for the Kamakura government was actually in serious trouble. The bureaucracy would continue to function for another twenty-five years, but the system itself was moribund, a victim of the Mongol attacks. There had never been a national system of taxation, and consequently there was no means of paying for the war. This was an ultimately fatal dilemma for the shogunate, which was based upon the exchange of fealty for spoils. When the Hōjō regents found themselves unable to reward loyal service with lands or bounty, the bonds between lord and vassal began to loosen.

By the year 1300, Heian-kyō had become a city of persistent political intriguing. In the absence of effective control from the weakened administration at Kamakura, the long-dormant imperial line had become embroiled in a series of factional disputes, with as many as five ex-emperors maneuvering for control over the succession. Over the next two or three decades these contending factions gradually drew into two camps. In an ill-advised attempt to resolve the dispute and restore their flagging prestige, the Hōjō threw their support to one camp — just as the other, represented by Emperor Go-Daigo, was establishing itself. To make matters worse, the commander of the Hōjō troops, Ashikaga Takauji, defected to Go-Daigo's side even as he marched upon the capital in 1333 — a move that triggered widespread revolt among the samurai themselves. That summer the troops that had flocked to Go-Daigo's banner moved against Kamakura. Good soldiers to a man, the Hōjō regent and his attendants committed *seppuku* to avoid capture, while smoke from their burning city darkened the sky.

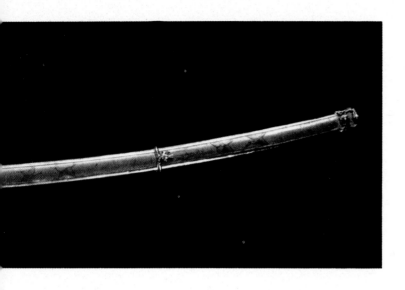

Determined to win by force the recognition that his
envoys had been unable to secure through negotiation,
China's Great Khan, Kublai, launched a massive seaborne
invasion of Japan in the fall of 1274 (above). As soon as
the Mongol fleet put ashore in northern Kyushu, it was
set upon by local samurai armed with longswords (top).

IV
The Court Eclipsed

Led by the turncoat Ashikaga Takauji, the armies avowing loyalty to Emperor Go-Daigo had overthrown the Kamakura shogunate in 1333 and returned national administrative control to Kyoto. Principal credit for the coup clearly belonged to Takauji, a fact that everyone except the emperor seemed willing to accept. Misconstruing the meaning of the victory that had been achieved in his name, the misguided puppet monarch became convinced that he personally could restore effective imperial rule to Japan after a hiatus of almost five centuries. For a time Takauji was willing to support Go-Daigo's anachronistic schemes, for they served to further his own ambitions — which were nothing less than to assume the shogunate. The victorious army commander, who was as pragmatic as the emperor was visionary, soon wearied of his former ally's naïve scheming, however, and in January, 1337, he drove Go-Daigo from Kyoto, replacing him with a more tractable member of the imperial family. The deposed emperor fled southward with his retinue, settling finally at Yoshino in the mountains south of Nara. There he established a rival court that spent the next sixty years pressing its claim to the throne — a claim enhanced by the fact that Go-Daigo's government-in-exile possessed the true imperial regalia, whereas the puppet court in Kyoto derived its legitimacy from forged copies.

This period, which Japanese historians call *Nambokuchō*, the Age of the Northern and Southern Dynasties, has been characterized as a "desperate prelude" to the uneasy rule of the Ashikaga shoguns that followed. The focus of the age was upon the contending dynasties, but the real contest in fourteenth-century Japan was not between rival emperors but between rival feudal lords — and what was contested was not titles, but land. For while the Northern and Southern courts were maneuvering for control of a powerless and impoverished throne, the provincial barons who had risen to prominence when the Kamakura shogunate fell were consolidating their power over extensive, tax-rich holdings in areas far from the capital. The royal contest captured the popular imagination, but it was the massive redistribution of feudal privilege that enabled the provincial lords ultimately to capture the seat of power.

The issue of the succession was finally resolved in 1392, and Go-Daigo's heirs returned to Kyoto with the understanding that their line would henceforth rule alternately with the line promoted by Ashikaga Takauji. However, through a combination of Ashikaga duplicity and imperial ineffectuality, no descendant of Go-Daigo ever sat upon the reunited Japanese throne. Takauji, for his part, proved no more successful in establishing a unified national government than Go-Daigo had been in reestablishing a strong monarchy. Instead, he and his fifteen Ashikaga successors were to preside over a nation wracked by civil discord that regularly imperiled the security of the shogunate itself. Their uncertain authority, never national in scope, was to become increasingly circumscribed with each passing decade — until, by the late fifteenth century, it could not really be said to extend much beyond the gates of the shogun's villa.

Like the Minamoto shoguns before them, the Ashikaga were to be supplanted by a more vigorous and effective political force. The difference, of course, was that in the latter case victory belonged not to a rival faction but to members of a new feudal society, one

composed of provincial governors and constables appointed during the Kamakura period, managers of the great tax-exempt manors of the Fujiwara era, and disaffected warlords. The members of this new class were known collectively as *daimyō,* or "great names."

The rise of the daimyo in the middle decades of the fourteeenth century was achieved at the expense of the Kyoto aristocracy, which had long been dependent upon the tax revenues generated by the outlying estates that the daimyo were gradually usurping. Deprived of this source of income, the imperial household suddenly found its existence imperiled. One fifteenth-century emperor was reduced to selling samples of his elegant calligraphy to support himself, and another, who died in 1500, lay unburied for six weeks while the imperial family raised funds to cover the expense of his funeral. (His successor went uncrowned for twenty-one years because the imperial treasury could not sustain the cost of a royal investiture.) The long decline of the Japanese imperial household had entered its most humiliating phase. Nouveau riche provincial boors taunted the emperor in the streets of his capital — and the divine descendant of the sun goddess wept openly over these insults to his once-revered line and over his utter helplessness in the face of them.

The capital was not without guidance in these unsettled times, however, for as Reischauer has noted, "with the financial eclipse of the court aristocracy cultural leadership in the capital city of Kyoto naturally passed to the shogun's court." It is more as art patrons than as politicians that the Ashikaga shoguns are remembered. The first of these cultural arbiters was Yoshimitsu, who assumed the shogunate in February,

1369, and governed with considerable effectiveness for the next twenty-six years.

At the time of Yoshimitsu's accession, three factors were beginning to radically reshape Japanese civilization. The first of these forces was unleashed by the daimyo themselves, who by mid-century were gravitating to the capital in increasing numbers. Once in Kyoto they developed an understandable craving for the trappings of aristocratic life — a combination of envy, curiosity, and enchantment that was to spark the final fusion of court aesthetics and feudal sensibilities and mark the emergence of a new governing class.

The second influence was China. Contacts with the mainland, never wholly interrupted even during the collapse of the T'ang dynasty, had mounted steadily since the dissemination in Japan of Zen Buddhism in the first decades of the thirteenth century. In part this renewed interest in China was encouraged by the daimyo, whose enthusiasm for the elegant, the iconoclastic, and the novel found a logical outlet in the acquisition of Chinese-made goods. It was also in part encouraged by the Ashikaga, who profited handsomely from such officially encouraged trade and who used those profits to underwrite lavish building projects, particularly in the quarter of Kyoto that gave its name to the age — the Muromachi.

The third, and unquestionably the most influential, of these forces was Zen Buddhism, which had become so solidly entrenched in the century and a half since the sect's formal establishment that it qualified as the nation's de facto state religion. The qualities that gave Zen its widespread appeal — its lack of encumbering dogma, its rejection of pomp and cant — also served to

free Zen priests of the ecclesiastical strictures that hampered members of other Buddhist sects, permitting Zen monks to participate actively in all phases of the capital's secular life. According to G. B. Sansom, the monks' services were desperately needed in fourteenth-century Kyoto, for the capital was ruled by ex-soldiers, men who displayed "a characteristic military inability to grasp the rudiments of civil administration." They were, therefore, "very much in the hands of astute and learned clerics" — who served the Ashikaga shoguns as legal advisers, accountants, and ambassadors.

It was these monks who had encouraged the resumption of trade with China, suggesting to Takauji that such expeditions could reap enormous profits — and that those profits, applied to the construction of a great new Zen temple on the outskirts of Kyoto, might placate the restless spirit of Go-Daigo, who had recently died in exile. The Chinese, who had no particular interest in trade with Japan but who were interested in ridding their shores of Japanese pirates, consented to permit limited trade in exchange for Japan's promise to suppress the brigands. Accordingly, a treasure ship set sail for the mainland in 1342, inaugurating a new era of trade that would flood China with Japanese fans, folding screens, lacquerware, and — most prized of all — fine-tempered swords. Copper, another Japanese export, eventually found its way back to the islands in the form of copper coins, minted in China but used as the regular medium of exchange in Japan in the Ashikaga period. With those coins the citizens of Kyoto were able to purchase such coveted Chinese exports as textiles, paintings, books, and drugs.

Trade with the mainland was so profitable — cargoes

sold in China for at least five times their domestic worth — that the shogun was able to placate the wraith of Go-Daigo in imperial style. Tenryū-ji, the temple complex that Takauji established at Arashiyama, was not only the largest aggregate of buildings in the sector but also one of the principal centers of Zen Buddhist activity in the entire region. With Nanzen-ji, the headquarters of the powerful Rinzai Zen Sect, it established a style that was to dominate religious architecture for centuries. In both precincts unpainted, untreated wood was combined with stark, whitewashed plaster to produce tangible, large-scale object lessons in the Zen principles of simplicity, purity, and unpretentiousness.

Encouraged by the success of these early missions, the shogunate pressed for wider trading privileges — which, in 1402, it obtained in exchange for a promise to eradicate the pirates that still plagued China's coastal waters. As good as their word, the shogun's forces promptly fell upon the pirate strongholds in the Korean Strait, rounded up a boatload of hostages, and shipped them off to Peking. And when the Chinese emperor, satisfied by this expression of the shogun's good intentions, returned the captives, the Japanese boiled them alive.

The Chinese insisted upon viewing all Japanese export items as tribute that was, at least in theory, destined for the emperor, and they acknowledged these offerings with reciprocal gifts. The Japanese, who soon discovered that these "gifts" regularly exceeded their "tribute" in value, readily acquiesced to the charade despite the implied insult to their national honor. By the beginning of the fifteenth century, the China trade was not only supporting the high-living shogun and his court — and, in the process, further enriching the already wealthy Zen temples of Kyoto — it was also handsomely rewarding dozens of lesser nobles and tradesmen who had performed small services in exchange for small percentages of profit. This sudden affluence spurred the growth of a vigorous merchant class, which led in turn to the development of merchant guilds and the expansion of Japan's port cities.

The great Zen temples of Kyoto, led by Nanzen-ji, used their profits from the China trade to revitalize and extend the nation's first system of popular education. These small, provincial church schools were generally staffed by Zen monks. The same was true of Ashikaga College, which was recognized for more than a century as the foremost center of classical Chinese learning in Japan. Predictably, the nobles of the Ashikaga court lavished their profits from the China trade on less selfless pursuits. Like their Venetian contemporaries, who were also enjoying unparalleled wealth from expanded overseas trade, the merchant princes of Kyoto had given themselves over to extravagance and ostentation. Led by the Ashikaga shogun Yoshimitsu, who clad himself in Chinese brocades and rode through the streets of the capital in a Ming-dynasty palanquin, these parvenu aristocrats restored to Kyoto the vibrant color that had largely faded with the downfall of the Fujiwara some three centuries earlier.

Unlike the Fujiwara, the Ashikaga could not draw upon the tax revenues of the entire nation to finance their building schemes, nor could they conscript peasant laborers to give those schemes form. On their limited budget a systematic rebuilding of the capital was impossible, but Yoshimitsu did manage to add a number of impressive structures to Kyoto nonetheless,

Fire-plagued Shōkoku-ji, which ranks second among Kyoto's five major Rinzai Zen temples, supplied the Ashikaga shogunate with a succession of worldly and capable advisers. It also supplied the world of art with a succession of extremely talented painters — beginning with Josetsu, a native-born artist who was deeply influenced by Sung dynasty themes and styles. Working with ink and water alone — a technique known as sumi-e — *Josetsu created this study of the founders of Buddhism, Taoism, and Confucianism during the early 1400's.*

among them the fire-plagued Zen temple of Shōkoku-ji, whose chief priests regularly served as advisers to the shogunate. In 1378, the twentieth year of Yoshimitsu's reign, the Hana-no-gosho, or Palace of Flowers, was completed to the shogun's exacting specifications. This most sumptuous of residences was used only briefly by Yoshimitsu — principally to entertain the emperor — for in 1395 he chose to relinquish his title and settle into nominal retirement outside the city.

The spot that Yoshimitsu chose for that purpose, the country estate of a Kamakura-era nobleman, was as appealing a site as Byōdō-in, and the retirement villa that he erected there quite literally outshone any building constructed in Kyoto since the completion of the great Phoenix Hall. Reflecting the cosmopolitan atmosphere of the times, the building's design was an amalgam of Chinese and Japanese elements. Reflecting the ex-shogun's love of the resplendent, the building was covered, both inside and out, in gold leaf. Once part of a larger complex, Kinkaku-ji, the Golden Pavilion, now stands alone on the lip of an artfully landscaped pond in a heavily wooded park northwest of Kyoto. It is, with good reason, the most famous structure in the capital, for it combines a superb natural setting with an airy, eclectic design refulgent in almost any light.

As a summer house Kinkaku-ji might be thought ambitious, but as an official residence — which, for all intents and purposes, it was — the structure is modest indeed. Its first floor, Japanese in style, contains the reception rooms where Yoshimitsu is said to have negotiated trade agreements with Ming ambassadors. The second floor, with its Chinese detailing, was the scene of Yoshimitsu's frequent tea parties and musicales. The

villa's third floor, which contains but a single room almost certainly used as the shogun's private chapel, seems to pierce the structure's gently arching roof, carrying the whole building's weight upward to the peak, which is crowned with a gilt bronze phoenix, symbol of a retired emperor.

On his death, Yoshimitsu left instructions that his retirement villa be converted into a Zen temple, a gesture that reflected not only the belated piety of the donor, but also the degree to which this remarkable sect had permeated and influenced every level of Japanese society. Zen Buddhism's impact upon the arts was everywhere in evidence, but nowhere was the evidence more dramatic — or the involvement more absolute — than in the field of painting.

At a time when native Japanese painters were creating vividly colored and frenetically detailed historical scrolls, Chinese Sung dynasty artists had turned to far simpler subject matter, which they treated in a monochromatic fashion with ink and wash. Japanese monks first encountered this new style, which they called *sumi-e,* or "ink painting," in the course of their increasingly frequent trips to the Zen monasteries of southern China, and it was they who introduced *sumi-e* to their native land. Zen, which rejected the worship of idols and thereby obviated the traditional Buddhist art forms, encouraged the development of *sumi-e,* which seemed a fitting means of recreating the likenesses of each temple's patriarchs. It was only a small step from such portraiture to landscape painting, and during the first decades of the fifteenth century two monks attached to Shōkoku-ji made the transition.

Josetsu and his pupil Shūbun were copyists, however,

turning out imitations of Sung dynasty landscapes, and they are remembered chiefly for having introduced *sumi-e* techniques to Sesshū, whom many historians consider the greatest of all Japanese painters. Sesshū, who had come to Kyoto as a youth, journeyed to China in 1467 at the midpoint of his long and productive career — during his visit he was purportedly asked to decorate one of the rooms in the new Ming palace in Peking. Kyoto had been engulfed by civil war in the artist's absence, and upon his return he resettled in western Honshu, where many of his surviving works are thought to have been created.

Perhaps the most famous of Sesshū's extant paintings is a fifty-five-foot-long scroll depicting the changing seasons, beginning with springtime and concluding with winter. Created in 1486 when the artist was sixty-six years old, the scroll reveals a range of brushwork, a penchant for innovation, and a subtlety of detail that few artists would have dared to attempt — or hoped to achieve — with ink and brush alone. A virtuoso exercise in sure and sustained creative energy, this work was to alter the history of Japanese art, eclipsing all existing schools and stamping the fifteenth century as the age of *sumi-e*. Indeed, so pervasive was Sesshū's influence that the greatest painter of the following century, Hasegawa Tōhaku, declined to put his own name to his works, preferring instead to style himself "Sesshū of the Fifth Generation."

In rather startling contrast to the scroll of the seasons, the kakemono, or hanging scroll, that Sesshū completed in 1496 as a parting gift for his pupil Shūen is soft and diffuse, its forms amorphous and floating. Working with a very wet brush in the style known as "splashed ink," the master has deftly suggested the essential elements in a fictive landscape. The economy of the brushwork, the almost mundane simplicity of the subject matter, and the reliance upon large areas of undefined space all reflect the influence of Zen Buddhism upon the artist and upon the age.

Zen, so frequently discussed in terms of its philosophical impact upon fifteenth-century Japan, underlay a far more important revolution, this one in aesthetics, that occurred simultaneously. Subsequent generations of Japanese might revile and pervert Zen teachings, but few could escape the effects of the sect's impact upon their culture. Landscape gardening, flower arranging, Nō drama, haiku and waka verse forms, the tea ceremony — all reflected a culture suffused with Zen precepts. From the beginning the Japanese had been predisposed to favor Zen, which had proved so compatible with their culture in the thirteenth century. And by the fifteenth century the two had become inextricable.

The results of this aesthetic revolution are evident in all sections of Kyoto, including the two most famous Muromachi-era gardens in the city — Saihō-ji and Ryōan-ji. The former, which is planted with some fifty varieties of luxuriant mosses, is internationally famous as Kokedera, the Moss Temple; the latter, composed of raked white gravel into which fifteen stones have been set apparently at random, is perhaps the most instantly recognizable garden in the entire world. The one is lush, the other arid; the first artfully mimics nature, the second seems to defy natural order. Yet these polar opposites strive to achieve the same end: to disengage the viewer from the familiar and secure, to oblige him to recreate the order of things from the

limited elements at hand. Both are dramatic departures from the norm, albeit in opposite directions — experimental forms, but perfect in themselves.

These two extremes, the lush and the arid, combine in the remarkable garden of Daisen-in at Daitoku-ji, where the lengendary Sōami, master landscape architect of the Muromachi era, created not one but two tiny gardens in a space less than one hundred feet long and perhaps twelve feet wide. Within these cramped confines he artfully arranged rocks, gravel, and a minimum of vegetation to create the illusion not only of limitless space but also of the whole of nature. The smaller of the two gardens distills the familiar landscape of Japan into a half-dozen shrubs and as many massive boulders. The other, a true rock garden in the style of Ryōan-ji, which Sōami is also credited with designing, recreates the unseen landscapes of China with raked gravel and a dozen stones. Here landscape gardening, like *sumi-e* painting, reduces nature to its simplest elements, allowing the viewer's imagination to color the black-and-white landscape as he chooses, creating mountains and snowfields, ponds and waterfalls.

In a sense, this same notion of viewer participation is embodied in Japan's arcane theater form, Nō drama. Probably an outgrowth of *sangaku* — a form of entertainment, dating at least from the eighth century, that originally combined acrobatics, juggling, and folk dancing — Nō began as little more than antic posturing in period costumes. The transformation of this street theater into a refined diversion worthy of the most aristocratic tastes is an achievement attributed to a Shinto priest named Kanami, who was born in the same year that Ashikaga Takauji entered Kyoto in tri-

umph. Around the year 1380, Kanami, an inventive and mercurial actor, and his son Seami, an unusually handsome young producer, were invited to Yoshimitsu's court. Whether the invitation reflected the bisexual shogun's appetite for drama or for young men has never been altogether clear, but the father and son team did thrive in the imperial capital — and so, as a consequence, did Nō.

The text of Nō dramas, if text it can fairly be called, was a sophisticated pastiche of contemporary verse set to music. Its uniqueness lay in the complex interrelationships between the chanted verse, the accompanying music, and the players' movements. It has been said that dance is the dominant element in Nō drama, and that all else is ancillary. This is true only in the sense that dance means choreography, for the motions themselves are frequently slow and attenuated, obliging the viewer to supply the action that the gestures only suggest. The spectator is likewise obliged to interpolate emotions, for the actors wear the expressive but frozen masks that a noted art critic has called "one of the most exquisitely developed genres in all of Japanese art history." Thus it must be said that the attraction of Nō lies not in the drama itself but in this theatrical form's elegant synthesis of Muromachi tastes.

"Everywhere there is a careful avoidance of the trite, the obvious, the emphatic," Sansom notes in his discussion of Nō. "The most powerful effects are those which are obtained by allusion, suggestion and restraint. . . ." This description might almost be taken as an epitaph for the age, and it unquestionably applies to the last great Ashikaga structure, the retirement villa built by the shogun Yoshimasa in Higashiyama, Kyoto's Eastern

Hills, in the 1480's. It had been Yoshimasa's original
intention to have the villa's chapel coated with silver
gilt, and although the shogun's ambition was never
achieved, the name — Silver Pavilion — persists. The
building itself is less ornate than Kinkaku-ji and has
but two floors, the lower Japanese in design, the upper
Chinese. It sits in a scaled-down garden purportedly
laid out by Sōami, and it is ringed by the dense forests
of Higashiyama. Near it stand the shogun's personal
quarters, which include a tiny, nine-foot-square tea-
room, said to be the first of its kind and the prototype
for all future teahouses. The living quarters themselves
are as innovative in style as the Silver Pavilion is derivative and include such pioneering architectural elements as *shōji* — sliding screens of translucent rice
paper — and a *tokonoma,* or display alcove. In fact, this
rather modest structure is the acknowledged forerunner
of Japan's distinctive domestic architecture.

In this secluded retreat Yoshimasa was to entertain
a coterie of fellow aesthetes in an atmosphere as surreal,
self-absorbed, and detached as that which enveloped
Heian-kyō in the last days of the Fujiwara period. In
the words of historian John Whitney Hall, Yoshimasa
"exemplified the courtly ineffectiveness to which the
shogun was eventually relegated." But Hall also ob-
serves that the seventh Ashikaga shogun was the "foremost patron of one of the most creative periods of cultural flowering in medieval Japan" — precisely because
he was unencumbered by political obligations. At the
center of the shogun's court was a monk named Nōami,
grandfather of the landscape gardener Sōami. A con-
noisseur of both Chinese and Japanese art, Nōami devoted his first months with Yoshimasa's entourage to

cataloging the shogun's private art treasures. Nōami's expertise, and consequently his influence, extended to other fields, however, and before long the monk was instructing the shogun in the writing of verse, *sumi-e* painting, and the tea ceremony.

The significance of this last course of instruction cannot be overemphasized, for in many ways the tea ceremony has come to symbolize the quintessence of Zen aesthetics and Muromachi refinement. It was Murata Shukō, a contemporary of Nōami's, who gave formal structure to this most Japanese of social rituals. He conceived of the tea ceremony as a contemplative interlude, one that began with a select group of guests gathering under an open pavilion in their host's garden. There they were met by the tea master, who led both host and guests to the teahouse — where the master prepared and served powdered green tea while the guests discussed a work of art from the host's collection.

The rapid growth of the cult of tea in the late Muromachi period necessitated the acquisition of ceremonial implements, and this in turn encouraged the development of such native crafts as textile manufacture, ironmongery, and the production of lacquerware and ceramics. The shogun's own collection of tea ceremonial implements, assembled with the assistance of Shukō and Nōami, achieved such fame that its contents are known to this day as "Higashiyama pieces." The premier piece in the collection was a four-inch-high brown-glaze ceramic bowl that was of unspectacular appearance but intriguing origin: according to acknowledged authorities, it was brought from China in 1227 by Dōgen, aristocratic cofounder of the Zen Buddhist Sect in Japan.

No subsequent ruler of Japan would approach Yoshimasa in refinement, but then perhaps none wanted to. All could see the terrible dangers inherent in such desperate neglect of official duty. Yoshimasa himself was to die in his beloved Higashiyama retreat in 1490, serenely untroubled by the civil war that had splintered the nation into more than sixty warring principalities. The buildings of Yoshimasa's retirement compound — which by 1483, the year the villa was officially completed, included an even dozen teahouses — faced the wooded slopes of the Eastern Hills. To the west lay Kyoto, which half a century of mob rule, climaxed by the apocalyptic feudal struggle known as the Onin War, had reduced to a charred, depopulated ghost town.

The most aristocratic of Japan's ancient theater forms, Nō drama, is said to have evolved out of the roistering public entertainments that were popular at the time Kyoto was founded. Originally little more than antic posturing in period costumes, Nō was to develop into an art form of extraordinary aural and visual splendor. By the sixteenth century these elaborately choreographed productions — set to chanted verse and performed alfresco — were drawing sizable audiences (right). The players wore exquisitely embroidered kimono (above) that were themselves works of art. Wooden face masks, carefully carved to suggest indeterminate emotion, were worn to reinforce the Lyric Drama's emphasis on nuance and gesture. Blackened teeth, artificial eyebrows, and chalk-white make-up identify the features seen in triplicate at upper right as belonging to a court lady of the late Fujiwara period.

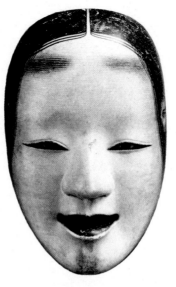

V

Japan's Three Heroes

Like Europe's Hundred Years' War, the Onin War in Japan, which involved two rival branches of the Ashikaga clan and their supporters, began as a war of succession. For the decade 1467 to 1477, the focus of that struggle was Kyoto, but within a few years the conflagration engendered by it had spread to every province in the nation and involved every daimyo. By 1600, those wars had run their course: the Ashikaga line had been extinguished, the capital had been leveled by fires and repeated assaults, and the social structure of Japan had been radically realigned. The form the last of these assumed during the final years of the anarchic *Sengoku Jidai* — the Age of the Country at War — would endure, virtually unchanged, until well into modern times.

This new social order was odds-on the most crucial outgrowth of the Onin War and its aftermath, for it meant the dissolution of the system of land tenure that had been in effect, with periodic modifications, since the eighth century. From before the time of Emperor Kammu, Japan's arable land had been parceled out in an arbitrary and haphazard manner to victorious generals, court favorites, disputatious nobles, and potentially troublesome junior members of the imperial family. In general, these *shōen*, or largely tax-exempt provincial estates, had been terrae incognitae — both to the ruler who granted them in fief and to the subjects who received them. Culturally as well as geographically remote from the capital, these great manors were seldom visited by the aristocrats of Kyoto, who were content to entrust the management of their *shōen* to others as long as they were supplied with a percentage of the revenues.

Few *shōen* were confined to a single geographical area, and fewer still were readily defensible. As long as the government in Kyoto exercised control over the nation as a whole, the question of defense remained academic, but with the gradual weakening of central authority during the Late Heian period, the frailty of the system became self-evident. The managers of these estates, joined by the authorities who had been appointed during the Kamakura period to prevent such acts of usurpation, had wrested control of many *shōen* from their nominal masters in Kyoto. Nor did the violent redistribution of the nation's most productive acreage end there, for these petty barons soon turned on one another. The piecemeal reduction of Japan's great daimyo and the gradual consolidation of their holdings was to be the central feature of the *Sengoku Jidai* — and in that light the Onin War can be seen as an early round in the match that ultimately pitted all the great feudal houses against one another. In 1467, at the outbreak of that war, the roughly two hundred and sixty daimyo in existence controlled two-thirds of the nation; by 1600, less than a dozen of the old feudal houses remained, competing for territory and authority with a like number of new houses. The surviving members of the old order were, by and large, confined to the west and northwest, beyond the reach of the aggressive new masters of Japan, daimyo who were to shape the nation's history for the next two and a half centuries.

This sweeping transformation of the country's social structure was one of the most profound in Japanese history. G. B. Sansom has observed that, "So far as concerns the personnel of her dominant classes, Japan was entirely refashioned by the year 1600." For the

better part of the sixteenth century, however, the national hierarchy was without a topmost stratum, for neither the emperor nor the Ashikaga shogun could exert any real influence over the daimyo. The consolidation of feudal power in the hands of a single paramount military and political figure would not come until the closing decades of the century, but then it would come with a rush. In the space of twenty years, three extraordinary men — the "three heroes" of early modern Japanese history — would crush the collective power of the daimyo, eliminate the threat that certain Buddhist sects had long posed to legitimate secular authority, and lay the foundations of a feudal society that would endure well into the 1800's.

The first of Japan's three heroes was Oda Nobunaga, the son of a minor feudatory from the Owari district. While still in his twenties, Nobunaga had dramatically expanded his family's holdings in Owari and several neighboring provinces through a shrewd combination of force and suasion, siege and marriage. The brilliant young tactician was only thirty — and poised for an attack on the capital — when he received an appeal for aid from Emperor Ogimachi. At the time, Nobunaga's forces had advanced to within a day's forced march of Kyoto, and the sovereign was eager to form a hasty alliance with the strongest of the feudal powers ranged against him.

Nobunaga declined the emperor's initial entreaty, concentrating instead upon the formation of a network of alliances to protect his flanks against surprise attack. But by the time Ogimachi's second plea was issued in 1567, Nobunaga was ready to make his bid for supreme national power. Ashikaga Yoshiteru, great-grandson of

Yoshimasa, had recently committed *seppuku* in the wake of a particularly brazen rebel attack on the capital. The marauders had slashed their way to the heart of the city and set fire to the shogun's palace itself, and Yoshiteru had chosen to die amid the flaming ruins rather than face the indignity of capture. The hapless shogun's brother, Yoshiaki, had taken refuge outside the city, where he remained until 1568, when he marched back into Kyoto in the train of Nobunaga's 30,000-man army. With order restored, Yoshiaki was able to assume his place as shogun, although he was in fact but an instrument of Nobunaga's ambitions.

Aided by a handful of faithful retainers, among them Toyotomi Hideyoshi, Nobunaga next set about to secure the home provinces — and by 1573 he had largely achieved that objective. His power base established, Nobunaga shed the pretense that he was acting on Yoshiaki's behalf and drove the last Ashikaga shogun from Kyoto, assuming the office himself. By this time Nobunaga had begun to work toward another of his primary objectives — the systematic destruction of the great Buddhist monasteries that had bullied and blackmailed the capital for centuries. He was well advised to do so, for by the middle of the sixteenth century the Tendai monastery of Enryaku-ji alone maintained a standing army that ranked among the most powerful in the nation.

In the course of the fifteenth century, as the Ashikaga shoguns had gradually forsworn public obligation for private diversion, the monks of Mount Hiei had correspondingly insinuated themselves into the resulting political vacuum. The authority of the shogun had become so shadowy by 1536, for instance, that troops

The Sengoku Jidai, *Japan's equivalent of the Hundred Years' War, was marked by the violent redistribution of most of the nation's arable land. This upheaval led to the formation of autonomous agrarian groups and to widespread communal harvesting. The painting seen at left records the ceremonies attending one such collaborative effort — the transplanting of young rice shoots. To the strains of* dengaku, *"the music of the fields," men in rush skirts carry bundled plants to kimono-clad women who set them out in the paddies.*

from Enryaku-ji were able to mount a massive campaign against the rival Nichiren Sect in Kyoto, slaughtering hundreds of priests and razing every Nichiren temple in the capital. Buoyed by their success, the armed priests of Hiei grew self-confident and incautious. Several of their less timely mid-century assaults on the capital were repulsed, and the priests were driven back into the dense forests of their sacred mountain. These were petty reverses, inconsequential in themselves but indicative of a far more serious problem that now plagued the monastery's leadership — the inability to assess the changing political climate accurately. In 1571 this shortsightedness led the monks to make a fatally foolish mistake: they took sides against Oda Nobunaga and his generals, who lost no time in surrounding the vast temple complex. Undaunted by Enryaku-ji's status as hallowed ground, Nobunaga ordered all three thousand buildings on the summit of Hiei put to the torch and all inhabitants put to the sword. When the entire mountaintop had been reduced to smoldering ruins, Nobunaga's troops withdrew. Orders were issued for the construction of a castle at the base of Hiei to guard against any further threats from the "Demon Quarter."

The small bastion that Oda Nobunaga's engineers erected at the foot of Mount Hiei was little more than a stone and timber garrison house, but it was the precursor of larger and much more lavish sixteenth-century structures. Indeed, this was so conspicuously an age of castle building that it takes its name, Momoyama, from one of the most famous of those structures. Nobunaga himself resided at Adzuchi Castle overlooking Lake Biwa, northeast of Kyoto. His fortress-residence, whose

wood and clay superstructure rested upon a stone base more than seventy feet high, was the largest structure thus far erected in Japan. Its design represented a radical departure from traditional styles, one dictated by the exigencies of contemporary warfare and influenced by Western architectural innovations. The two were in fact closely associated, for the Portuguese traders who had landed on the island of Tanegashima, south of Kyushu, in 1543 brought with them both the arquebus and the techniques of castle building. The introduction of the former was to necessitate the construction of the latter, triggering frenetic building programs in every province of Japan.

The Japanese were already familiar with gunpowder, of course; the Mongols had used it against them in the late thirteenth century. But until the mid-sixteenth century the sword remained the warrior's chief weapon. With the wholesale conversion to modern weaponry — first muskets, then field artillery — it was necessary to construct far sturdier redoubts than had previously been known. Castles similar to Adzuchi began to rise in all corners of the nation, built by provincial barons whose survival now clearly depended upon quarried stone as much as feudal alliances. These fortifications reflected the degree to which central authority had disintegrated under the Ashikaga. They also underscored the true nature of a new and rather grimly pragmatic system of land distribution that had come into being, one based upon force of arms rather than imperial or shogunal patents. Under this system, power radiated from the fortress of the feudal lord, diminishing progressively as it neared the borders of his domain. Security was a direct function of proximity to the fortress,

and as a result these bastions eventually became the commercial as well as political focuses of Japan. Prosperous new trading centers, among them Osaka, Hiroshima, Nagoya, and Edo — the future Tokyo — sprang up around these feudal keeps.

Pragmatism may have dictated the construction of Momoyama-era castles, but pure ostentation governed their decoration — with the result that Nobunaga's fortress at Adzuchi was the first such residence in Japanese history to reflect the tastes of its occupant rather than those of the Kyoto aristocracy. Zen aesthetics, so central to all aspects of Ashikaga life, held little appeal for the roughhewn Nobunaga, an implacable foe of the Buddhist priesthood. The decline of Buddhist art can be dated from the time of his accession. Nobunaga was no philistine, however, and under the patronage of this hegemon and his successors, artists of the Kanō family — long overshadowed by the disciples of Sesshū — were to achieve delayed public recognition.

Never in world history has a single family proved such a wellspring of talent — or so thoroughly dominated the aesthetic proclivities of an entire nation — as did the Kanō family. It has been said the influence of the family, which encompassed seven generations spanning two hundred years, was so pervasive that it endured for a century after the clan itself had died out. The Kanō style was a unique fusion of Sung-dynasty Chinese subject matter and traditional Japanese techniques, particularly the vivid *Yamato-e* style popularized during the Kamakura period. The resulting works of art, larger and brighter than any predecessors, reversed the trend toward naturalism and emphasized the decorative aspects of the subjects depicted. Often set against backgrounds of embossed gold leaf and outlined in black, these emphatically two-dimensional figures matched their surroundings in scale and force. Kanō Eitoku, whose vigorous brushwork suggests that he was trained in ink painting in his youth, executed vibrant polychromatic paintings for every public room in Adzuchi Castle, but shifted to delicate monochromes for Nobunaga's chambers. His efforts both softened and glamorized the military stronghold, giving Adzuchi Castle an aura of elegance belying its actual function.

Japan's ruling elite, which had responded to the introduction of firearms by erecting Western-style fortifications like Adzuchi, reacted with equal pragmatism to Portugal's second most significant export: Christianity. In all, this alien religion probably reached fewer than two per cent of the population, and there is reason to believe that many alleged converts viewed the new doctrine as nothing more than Buddhism in another guise. Indeed, it was demeanor rather than doctrine that most impressed the Japanese; in an age of widespread corruption among the Buddhist priesthood, the piety and probity of the Jesuit missionaries who began arriving in Kyushu in increasing numbers in the 1550's met with considerable favor.

The Society of Jesus was only a decade old in 1549, the year that Francis Xavier, one of the order's founders, landed on the south island. It was Xavier's earnest intention to preach to the masses, converting the nation from the bottom up, but he soon found the opposite approach more efficacious — and when Father Gaspar Vilela set out for Kyoto in 1559 it was with the express intention of meeting the shogun himself.

Three heroic figures were ultimately to emerge from the anarchy and nihilism of the Sengoku Jidai. *The first of these was Oda Nobunaga (right), who began the process of reuniting the war-wracked nation. The overweening symbol of Nobunaga's growing hegemony was Adzuchi Castle, a massive granite and timber redoubt overlooking Kyoto's Lake Biwa. Adzuchi has long since disappeared, and with it have vanished the brilliantly colored painted screens that once adorned its interior. These were the work of Kanō Eitoku, an artist of exceptional facility and boldness. Eitoku's talents are amply evident in such surviving works as the study of mythic leonine beasts at left.*

Father Vilela's account of his journey to the capital describes Kyoto as a city of some 96,000 dwellings, a figure that suggests considerable rebuilding had taken place in the aftermath of the Onin War, even in the absence of a comprehensive renovation scheme. (Much of this reconstruction had been undertaken by enterprising groups of townspeople operating through neighborhood committees known as *machi*.) Furthermore, if the Jesuit's estimate can be relied upon, Kyoto was supporting a population of half a million people in 1559, which made it larger than any city in sixteenth-century Europe.

Out of eagerness to please the Portuguese traders who brought the Jesuits to their shores, several petty lords of Kyushu would order their subjects to convert en masse. In exchange for such pro forma gestures they hoped to acquire special trading concessions. Kyoto would make no such accommodation, however, and Vilela's congregation was composed largely of social outcasts seeking nursing care, for which the Jesuits were renowned. In time the missionaries did succeed in converting a sizable group of Kyoto-area samurai, and in 1568 Vilela's successor, the famous mission historian Father Luis Frois, was received by Oda Nobunaga himself. The hegemon had little interest in Christian doctrines, but keen enthusiasm for the Western scientific developments with which the missionaries were conversant. He tolerated their ministry because he admired their discipline, valor, scholarship, and sense of superiority — in short, their samurai virtues.

The Japanese, who identified the Portuguese as *namban*, or "southern barbarians" — a reference to the direction from which the foreigners had approached the archipelago — were intrigued by the Europeans' physiognomy. This fascination is evinced in a unique body of art works, mostly folding screens, created during the late sixteenth and early seventeenth centuries and known collectively as Namban art. Superficially similar to the works of Kanō Eitoku and his contemporaries, these gilded, highly colored screens are peopled by pallid, spindle-legged "southern barbarians" with prominent noses and pointed beards.

Oda Nobunaga, whose patronage had encouraged the Christian mission in Japan, sponsored the Jesuit fathers for fourteen years — from his first audience with Frois in 1568 until his untimely death, at the hands of a disaffected vassal, in 1582. The indefatigable conqueror was only forty-eight when he was assassinated, and his dream of unifying Japan was only half realized.

The task of subduing the rest of the archipelago fell to Toyotomi Hideyoshi. The second of Japan's three heroes was a baseborn vassal who had become one of Nobunaga's most successful and most reliable field commanders. Hideyoshi, whose simian features and hyperkinetic personality had earned him the affectionate sobriquet Saru — "Monkey" — first met Nobunaga when the latter was only twenty. At the time, the eighteen-year-old Hideyoshi was pledged to another master, but he promptly severed those ties and threw in his lot with the charismatic young commander from Owari. The long, close association that developed between the future conqueror of Kyoto and his successor was to profit both enormously.

Within three years of Oda Nobunaga's death, Hideyoshi succeeded in having himself appointed *kampaku* — the first time in Japanese history that the regency

In 1549, a decade after their order was founded, members of the Society of Jesus established a missionary outpost on the island of Kyushu. The first Jesuits had come out of the South Seas, and consequently the Japanese called them namban, or "southern barbarians." The same term is used to identify the distinctive works of art — mostly folding screens — that were created during Japan's "Christian century." One of the most spectacular of these Namban screens is shown below. Both signed and sealed by Kanō Naizen, a member of the talented family that dominated Japanese art for more than three centuries, this heavily gilded folding screen depicts the departure of a Portuguese trading vessel.

had ever been awarded to a commoner. Having expressed fervent gratitude to the emperor for his elevation, Hideyoshi lost little time in carrying the war against the recalcitrant daimyo deep into their own territory, pitting a quarter of a million loyal troops against the massed might of the Shimazu clan, which by the end of 1586 had conquered almost all of Kyushu. His massive victory over the Shimazu was to be the penultimate act of the *Sengoku* drama.

Having subjugated Kyushu, Hideyoshi next moved to conquer the Kantō. The climax came with the capitulation of Odawara Castle in July of 1590. Peace and tranquillity were restored to the capital for the first time in more than a century. To guarantee that unity and harmony, Hideyoshi inaugurated a policy of burdensome but useful *sankin,* or public progresses, in the course of which the regent's ministers attempted to detect the least hint of unrest among his subjects. The wily Hideyoshi further ensured himself against latent conspiracies by taking hostages from the families of each of the major daimyo.

His national ambitions realized in the short space of eight years, Hideyoshi cast about for a new military objective — and soon settled upon the conquest of China. In 1592, an invasion army of 200,000 men crossed the Korean Strait and swiftly cut its way north as far as the Yalu River, where it encountered and obliterated a 5,000-man Chinese army. By January, 1593, a substantially larger Chinese army had put Hideyoshi's troops to flight, however, and the Japanese accepted a negotiated settlement. When the Chinese negotiators arrived in Japan, they carried with them an official communiqué from the Ming emperor.

His letter, which addressed Hideyoshi as the "King of Japan," was patronizingly effusive in its praise of the lowborn ruler, a calculated insult that infuriated the Japanese and spurred plans for a second invasion. That campaign, launched in 1597 with the limited objective of conquering only the Korean Peninsula, was cut short by Hideyoshi's death the following year. Leaderless and disheartened, the Japanese rapidly abandoned what would prove to be their last overseas military expedition until modern times.

Toyotomi Hideyoshi's seemingly boundless megalomania had served the Japanese better in domestic affairs than in foreign wars, and despite the brevity of his reign he remains one of the most colorful and influential figures in the nation's history. In retrospect, many of Hideyoshi's actions appear regressive in nature, but there is no question that he was intensely eager to establish an enduring central government. It was Hideyoshi, for example, who spearheaded the drive to impose upon sixteenth-century Japan the sort of rigid social distinctions that had characterized the Heian era, thereby ratifying and stabilizing the dramatic transformation of Japanese society that had occurred during the *Sengoku Jidai.* That a peasant who had risen to the top of the social order through his military prowess should initiate such a drive is undeniably ironic; that he should largely succeed is a tribute to his forcefulness and determination.

In pursuit of this goal, Hideyoshi instituted a series of *katanagari,* or "sword hunts," that began in 1588 with the double purpose of disarming possible insurgents and underscoring the class distinction between the farmer and the humbled samurai. To placate the disgruntled populace, Hideyoshi declared that the con-fiscated weapons would be smelted down and reshaped into bolts, braces, and nails, which would then be used in erecting a new Hall of the Great Buddha in Kyoto. "In the days of the emperor Shōmu," Hideyoshi declared, "it took twenty years to build the Daibutsu-den in Nara. I will build one in five years." Characteristically, Hideyoshi's plans called for the construction of a Buddha that would exceed even the great effigy at Nara in size — and that would be covered with lacquer made from 10,000 bags of powdered oyster shell. Several years and several sword hunts later, the huge temple was completed, but its future seemed clouded almost from the start. Destroyed by an earthquake in 1596, the year after its festive dedication, the temple was rebuilt in 1610–14. But when another earthquake struck in 1662, the irreparably damaged structure was pulled down and its central image used in the minting of coins.

Toyotomi Hideyoshi's building schemes were not confined to temple precincts or to Kyoto, and during his sixteen-year reign he ordered the construction of three sumptuous new residences. The first of these castles, Jurakudai, was located in Kyoto itself. The second stood atop Momoyama — "Peach Hill" — in Fushimi, south of the city. The last of his pleasure domes towered above the prospering port city of Osaka. Built by 30,000 laborers working around the clock for three solid years, Osaka Castle may well have been the largest structure in the sixteenth-century world. In any event it was the perfect architectural symbol of the age, for its tiled roofs and soaring eaves rested upon a base of cyclopean granite blocks — a representative fusion of the refined tradition of the Ashikaga era, the sturdy

practicality of the nation's self-made master, and the ebullience of Japan's Momoyama-period artists.

From the outside, Osaka Castle's white bulk must have struck visitors as forbiddingly austere. Inside, however, restraint gave way to polychromatic extrava-gance that was without precedent in the West. All wooden surfaces — beams, lintels, transoms, and the like — were intricately carved in deep relief, and the ceilings, sliding partitions, and folding screens that subdivided the castle's interior were covered with bril-liantly colored paintings or encrusted with gold leaf. In some instances, gold was used in place of plaster, and it was used throughout for locks, hinges, doorpulls, and other hardware. Piling excess upon excess, Hideyoshi commanded that articles destined for his personal use be fashioned out of gold as well.

Kanō Eitoku was engaged by Hideyoshi to oversee the embellishment of all three castles. In addition to countless *fusuma,* or sliding panels — most of which were lost in the wars of succession that followed Hide-yoshi's death — Eitoku is known to have contributed some one hundred pairs of folding screens to Momo-yama Castle alone. In part, Eitoku's extraordinary out-put can be attributed to the enormous straw brush that he used; in part, it must be attributed to the scale on which he worked. Both were unheard of in Japanese art history. The net effect was nothing less than spell-binding, as Sansom's walking tour through the corri-dors of Hideyoshi's gilded bestiary suggests:

On the walls, mostly of bright gold, there are blue-eyed tigers prowling through groves of bamboo, or multi-coloured *shishi* — mythical beasts like lions, but amiable and curly-haired — that gambol among peonies

*Toyotomi Hideyoshi (above), the baseborn
conqueror who oversaw the critical middle phase
of Japan's reunification, was not only a brilliant
battlefield tactician but also a dedicated master
builder. Under his aegis three enormous, lavishly
appointed palaces were constructed in the vicinity
of the capital. The first, Jurakudai, lay within the
city itself; the second, Momoyama, or "Peach Hill,"
Castle, stood on a rise south of Kyoto. The last,
Osaka Castle (left), may well have been the largest
structure in the sixteenth-century world, and it
was unquestionably the most splendidly decorated.*

against a golden background. There are gorgeous landscapes, thick with old pines and blossoming plum-trees, where bright birds perch on fantastic rocks or float amid ripples of deep blue. There are groves and banks and gardens, rich with brilliant leaves and flowers; bearded and sinuous dragons winding their complicated length through sepia clouds; gaggles of wild geese sweeping across the moon. . . .

Interestingly enough, the artist whom many authorities consider the supreme technician of the Momoyama period was not a member of the Kanō family at all, but rather, a disciple of the great ink painters of the Ashikaga era. Hasegawa Tōhaku styled himself "Sesshū of the Fifth Generation," and his works are indeed suffused with the master's posthumous influence. The famed *Monkeys* screen in the collection of Shōkoku-ji in Kyoto exemplifies the best features of the "splashed ink" style: soft, amorphous shapes suspended on an uncrowded canvas. These same attributes spill over into Tōhaku's polychrome works, notably the magnificent wall paintings preserved in a special museum attached to Chishaku-in in Kyoto. Commissioned by Hideyoshi to embellish the living quarters of Shōun-ji, a small temple erected in honor of his son and heir, Sutemaru, who was born in 1589 and died in 1591, these panels are among the most beautiful of all the works produced during the Momoyama period. Their composition, coloring, and decorative detail are without equal, and their state of preservation is nothing short of miraculous.

One of the enduring mysteries of the Momoyama period is why Hideyoshi, the most ostentatious ruler in Japanese history, should have patronized and befriended the sixteenth century's foremost advocate of

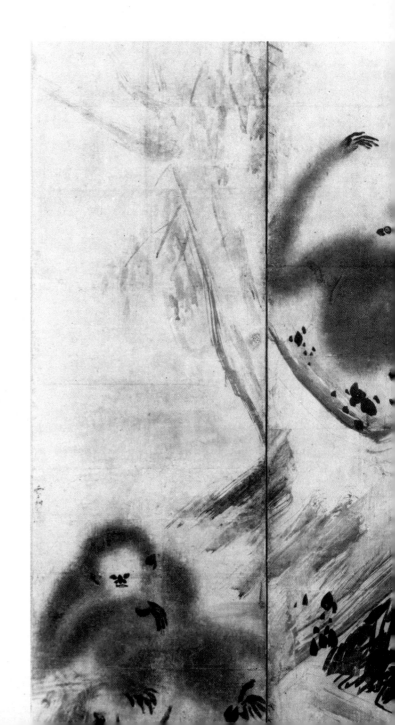

No sixteenth-century artist could match either the versatility or the virtuosity of Hasegawa Tōhaku, who worked with skill and grace in many media. His polychrome screens are considered elegant exemplars of Momoyama art, and his monochrome ink paintings are said to rival those of Sesshū. Tōhaku's debt to the legendary master of sumi-e *is evident in works such as the screen below, which combines soft forms with assertive brushwork.*

austerity and simplicity, the tea master Sen no Rikyū. No two personalities could have been more diametrically opposed, for Hideyoshi sought beauty in profusion whereas Rikyū found beauty in singularity. The extent of the two men's differences — and a clue to their interest in each other — is revealed in an oft-told and possibly apocryphal tale. Hideyoshi, an avid amateur horticulturist and flower fancier, had arranged to take tea with the master at a time when the latter's famed morning glories were certain to be in bloom. Thus it was to the hegemon's considerable dismay that he arrived at the appointed hour to find the garden surrounding Rikyū's teahouse stripped bare. The baffled guest was then led into the tea pavilion, where he found a single morning glory displayed in Rikyū's *tokonoma*. The master, who considered this bloom the essence of his garden, had personally picked and discarded all the other blossoms, lest they detract from the pleasure of viewing the chosen flower.

Sen no Rikyū's association with Toyotomi Hideyoshi was a curious one, for it paired the staunch advocate of simplicity with a man whose penchant for the grandiose knew almost no bounds. (Indeed, Hideyoshi is said to have asked Rikyū to design a teahouse of pure gold for his palace gardens.)

Rikyū himself looked upon the tea ceremony as a serene respite from mundane cares, and he urged practitioners of the tea ceremony to use the most pedestrian of utensils. Yet through his contact with Hideyoshi, Rikyū found himself acting as official adviser to the hegemon as the latter laid plans for the justly famous Kitano Tea Party, held in a wooded area on the city's outskirts in 1587. More nearly akin to a country fair

An avid amateur horticulturist, Hideyoshi staged many flower-viewing parties in Kyoto's famous gardens. The contemporary painting at right depicts an excursion to Daigo-ji undertaken in 1598, the year of Hideyoshi's death. It was on that very outing that the aging conqueror happened on the sadly dilapidated rural temple of Sambō-in. Restored and greatly enlarged upon Hideyoshi's orders, Sambō-in (below) was to become one of the premier scenic attractions in a city of notable gardens.

than anything else, Hideyoshi's ten-day fete featured music, dancing, and an exhibition of his personal art treasures. Invitations took the form of public announcements in Kyoto, Osaka, and other major cities, and thousands of ordinary citizens made the journey to the Kitano forest to take tea at any of eight hundred pavilions set up under Rikyū's close supervision. Critics have labeled the Kitano festival a gross distortion of a venerated and elevated social custom, and some have even accused Hideyoshi of intentionally perverting the spirit of the ceremony, once the exclusive province of Ashikaga aesthetes. What no one disputes is the democratizing influence of Kitano, which introduced *chadō*, "the way of tea," to all levels of Japanese society.

The uneasy alliance between the self-effacing tea master and the self-aggrandizing hegemon began to disintegrate after Kitano, and by 1591 the rift had become absolute: for reasons that are still disputed, Rikyū was ordered to commit *seppuku* by his disenchanted ruler. At roughly the same time Hideyoshi's heir-apparent died unexpectedly, leaving the fifty-five-year-old commander without male issue. In due course one of his younger concubines did produce another son, Hideyori, but this child was only five years old when his father died in 1598. Hideyoshi, who had risen to power by shunting aside Oda Nobunaga's infant son, was well aware of the perils his own son would face after his demise, and in his last years the hegemon did what he could to ensure the succession of his line. His efforts were to no avail, however: the five co-regents appointed to oversee Hideyori's minority soon turned on one another, briefly embroiling the nation in yet another civil war. This time the resolution was swift and decisive,

with victory going to Tokugawa Ieyasu, the last of Japan's three heroes, in the fall of 1600.

The battle of Sekigahara, which pitted Ieyasu's troops against the combined armies of his rivals, has rightfully been called "the most significant battle in Japanese history," for it marked the triumph of the new social order. The battle itself began at eight o'clock in the morning on October 21 and lasted well into the afternoon, by which time the rival barons were in full retreat. Three years later, Ieyasu was to establish a new shogunate, one based not in Kyoto but in the eastern region known as the Kantō. Within a decade of his move to the provincial village of Edo, Ieyasu was able to insist that the great daimyo all build residences within the walls of his compound, but it was not until 1614 that the new shogun felt strong enough to challenge Hideyoshi's son and putative heir.

Throughout this period, Hideyori and some 100,000 loyal supporters had holed up in the Osaka region, where they valiantly resisted a siege that achieved its objective in 1615 only because Ieyasu convinced Hideyori that he was anxious to conclude an armistice — and then used the respite from battle to bridge the castle's triple moat and storm the keep. Osaka Castle, the symbolic bulwark of the Momoyama state and the repository of many of its greatest cultural treasures, was set afire. And by the time those flames had been damped they had consumed the corpse of Hideyori, who had chosen suicide when it became obvious that his cause was lost. Hideyoshi's principal fortress — and his hopes of perpetuating his family's domination over Japan — lay in ruins; from them would rise a new national government, the first that could truly claim the name.

"Resting on the land cultivated by Nobunaga and sown by Hideyoshi," a Japanese adage avers, "Ieyasu enjoys a rich harvest." By and large, that harvest would be reaped in the east, where Ieyasu and his Tokugawa successors were to establish an independent military administration. Kyoto would remain the titular capital of Japan for better than two and a half centuries, but it would never again play a commanding role in the nation's political affairs.

Worst of all, perhaps, the citizens of the old imperial capital were obliged to tolerate the presence of an alien structure in the very heart of their city, a vast new shogunal palace built by Ieyasu. Nijo Castle, as this monument to Tokugawa suzerainty is known, was only briefly occupied by the last of Japan's three heroes, but it was maintained thereafter as an opulent reminder of the new ruling dynasty's unseen presence in Kyoto. That Nijo Castle was virtually unfortified, resembling in style the princely villas of the Ashikaga period rather than the granite redoubts of the Momoyama, was a further rebuke to the powerless populace of the capital.

The Tokugawa policy of demolishing or dismantling the castles erected by their predecessors has forced scholars to examine the structures built by Ieyasu in order to reconstruct the appearance of those erected by Nobunaga and Hideyoshi. Fortunately, Nijo Castle perpetuates both the architectural and the artistic traditions of the Momoyama age. As a matter of fact, the Karamon Gate, which opens onto the palace's entry court, is said to have come from Hideyoshi's Momoyama Castle itself. The principal structure, which is set toward the eastern edge of a seventy-acre compound and contains thirty-three rooms, has been described as "the most ornate, materialistic structure that a Japanese man ever created for himself." Its principal audience halls and waiting rooms were decorated in the early 1600's by junior members of the Kanō family. Kanō Tanyū, for example, was only twenty-five when he contributed genre scenes of pines, eagles, cheetahs, and tigers to the front reception rooms, and Kanō Naonobu was but twenty-two when he executed the wall paintings of cherry blossoms that enliven the chamber used by the shogun to greet his daimyo.

The progression from Nijo Castle's front gate through its great halls and into the private quarters that lie beyond is an artistic progression as well, for paintings play an important psychological role in the design of the palace. In the waiting rooms just inside the carriage gate, jungle cats prowl along the walls, their appearance no less ferocious for their having been drawn by artists who had never seen real tigers and were compelled to work from skins and imagination. The repository for the shogun's weapons is, appropriately, guarded by a malevolent eagle, but the hall of the daimyo — who were, in theory at least, utterly loyal to the shogun and therefore beyond intimidation — is free of such symbolic displays of power. The men who met there were well aware of the Tokugawas' absolute authority, and they were aware too that heavily armed samurai lurked behind the orange-tasseled sliding panels that flanked the shogun's dais.

It was only in the women's quarters that the vibrant palette of the Kanō school was abandoned for restful works executed in delicate pastels. Here the shogun could sit with his retainers and concubines, surrounded by a winter landscape punctuated with indistinct fig-ures of geese, herons, and other water birds. Here he was protected by loyal servants, dedicated samurai, and what is perhaps the most distinctive architectural feature of the age: Nijo Castle's famed "nightingale floors." Set upon specially designed metal braces that prevented direct contact between the floorboards and their supporting crossbeams, these walkways responded to the lightest footfall with telltale creaks and groans, alerting the shogun to any movement in the corridors outside his rooms.

Begun in the same year that Ieyasu moved his headquarters east to Edo — and completed in the year that the siege of Osaka Castle began — Nijo served the Tokugawa shoguns with decreasing frequency every year thereafter. The epicenter of national power had shifted permanently and emphatically to the east, to the city that was to evolve into the great metropolis of Tokyo, and there was less need with each passing year for the vital, aggressive Tokugawa to seek counsel from the lethargic and moribund Kyoto aristocracy.

The remains of Tokugawa Ieyasu, last of Japan's three heroes and founder of its greatest shogunal dynasty, are interred in a vast mausoleum at Nikkō, seventy-five miles north of modern Tokyo. This most famous of Tokugawa-period structures (left) offers irrefutable proof of the new regime's fondness for exterior adornment. Artisans imported from Kyoto applied six acres of gold leaf to Ieyasu's tomb and to its principal outbuildings, whose external surfaces are covered with intricate carvings (detail at right).

practice of their faith. The so-called General Persecution of Japan's Christian community had begun.

The systematic persecution of Christians gained impetus under Ieyasu's immediate successors, Hidetada and Iemitsu. The former was responsible for the Great Martyrdom of Nagasaki in 1622, in which fifty-five Christians were executed; the latter celebrated his accession in 1623 by ordering the Great Martyrdom of Edo, in which fifty Christians were burned at the stake. As this policy of extermination engulfed the nation, believers were lucky to be given the choice between martyrdom and apostasy. The surviving remnants of the Christian church worshiped covertly when they dared worship at all, and only the oldest centers of missionary activity, those located in Kyushu and western Honshu, continued to defy the government.

One such pocket of resistance was the Shimabara Peninsula, east of Nagasaki, where messianic fervor combined with resentment caused by unusually harsh taxation to create open rebellion in late 1637. Led by a charismatic youth of fifteen whom they hallowed as an angel descended from heaven, some 37,000 men, women, and children took refuge in a moldering castle on the Shimabara headland. There they held out for nearly four months against an army of over 100,000 men, suffering defeat only when they ran out of provisions. (Of their original number, only 105 survived the ensuing carnage.) Events appeared to have borne out the shogunate's suspicions — and, perhaps more importantly, they had reinforced the Tokugawa leadership's prejudice against foreigners. In the wake of Shimabara, the shogunate therefore adopted the policy of strict exclusionism that became the dominant political feature

of the Tokugawa era. For the next two centuries the nation's only contact with the West was through the port of Nagasaki. A restricted number of Dutch trading vessels was permitted to enter Nagasaki Bay each year, but these ships were obliged to tie up at Deshima Island, a man-made wharf and warehouse facility in the harbor, and crew members were expressly forbidden to set foot on shore.

With Buddhism suffering official opprobrium and Christianity official interdiction, the seventeenth-century Japanese found themselves turning to another great religion for solace and direction. This was Confucianism, a two-thousand-year-old guide to social behavior and proper government that fit only the broadest definition of religion. With its emphasis upon the primacy of group welfare and personal discipline, Confucianism appealed immensely to the Tokugawa, who were even then in the process of elaborating a national system of government based, like Confucianism, on the concept that a man's first duty was not to himself but to society as a whole.

Central to the neo-Confucian doctrine that gained widespread popularity in the first decades of Tokugawa rule was the belief that supreme political power could and should be entrusted to a single man, whose first obedience was to the Confucian moral order. Significantly, the Tokugawa saw themselves — and not the emperor — in that central role, and they sought to reinforce the concept of shogunal supremacy by elevating the founder of their line, Ieyasu, to divine status. To this end Iemitsu, the third Tokugawa shogun, ordered the construction of a vast new family tomb at Nikkō, seventy-five miles north of Edo. The Tōshōgū Mausoleum, which combines elements of the Shinto shrine, Buddhist temple, and hemispherical stupa tomb, carries the Momoyama penchant for polychrome embellishment to hyperbolic extreme. Sculptural excrescences cover every exposed surface with a riotous profusion of flora and fauna, real and mythical, and these are executed in brilliant shades of red, green, blue, and white, all touched with gold leaf.

During the same years that the Tokugawa were erecting their mausoleum at Nikkō, a totally different structural complex was rising in Kyoto, a building that stands today as mute testimony to the cultural schizophrenia of the age. Known as Katsura Rikyū, or the Katsura Detached Palace, this austerely elegant architectural masterpiece and its renowned gardens represent the apotheosis of a process of aesthetic refinement that began under the Ashikaga and reached definitive, small-scale expression in the rustic teahouses of Sen no Rikyū. By the early seventeenth century, this aesthetic had acquired a specialized vocabulary of virtually untranslatable words and phrases, the key terms being *wabi* and *sabi,* variously connoting restraint, simplicity, rustic character, and lack of artifice. Originally *wabi* had meant "sad," and *sabi,* "seemingly solitary" — in itself a rather subtle notion — but the words later took on other shades of meaning, some openly contradictory. The terms were said to imply a certain incompleteness or irregularity of design, an intentional asymmetry that was at once calculated and unrestrained.

The incongruous nature of this aesthetic, all but inexplicable in words, is manifest in structures such as Katsura Palace. Here subtleties of language give way to subtleties of design, and the byplay of language to the interplay of natural elements. Kenzo Tange, one of twentieth-century Japan's most distinguished architects, has expressed the contradictory nature of Katsura in these terms:

I see in it something of *Yayoi* culture — a definite, formal aesthetic, quiet, well-balanced, and dominated by a subjective, lyrical frame of mind. Still a force is always present in the palace which clashes with the traditional element. I think of this as the *Jomon* principle, the primitive life force of the Japanese race, an irrepressible vitality that invariably threatens to destroy formal aesthetics.

Significantly, the man who had commissioned Katsura Palace was Toyotomi Hideyoshi, the very epitome of irrepressible vitality. During the latter part of his rule Hideyoshi had formally adopted Prince Tomohito, younger brother of the emperor — a gesture designed to reconcile the peasant-conqueror and the crown. Kobori Enshū, a young architect who had already earned himself a considerable reputation in the capital, was retained to create suitable accommodations for Tomohito. According to popular legend, Enshū accepted Hideyoshi's commission on three conditions: first, that no ceiling be placed upon his expenses; second, that no completion date be imposed; and third, that no inspection tour of the grounds be staged until the entire project was completed. Ironically, this last provision — exacted to prevent the opinionated ruler from imposing his own views on the villa's design — prevented Hideyoshi from ever seeing the most noteworthy structure of the age, for the palace was not completed until half a century after his death.

The first Katsura Palace was used by Tomohito to

receive Emperor Go-Mizunoo in 1626. It subsequently passed into the hands of the prince's son, Tomotada, who engaged Enshū to add several new buildings to the complex in the 1630's. The grounds never exceeded fourteen acres, but they included a pond with five irregularly shaped islands and a garden that has been called the perfect synthesis of all previous Japanese gardening techniques. In truth, Katsura is a triumph of technique over substance, for its gardens are wholly man-made, the product of forty years of inspired landscaping and three centuries of assiduous maintenance.

The dimensions of that triumph are best appreciated by approaching the villa as guests of the owners once did, through a small side gate made of unpeeled oak logs and polished bamboo palings. (The main gate, which was opened only to the emperor, went unused for years at a stretch.) The path to the house was banked with closely planted shrubs and low trees whose presence prevented guests from glimpsing more than a tantalizing fragment of the gardens that lay beyond. Only after they had entered the old palace of Tomohito were visitors able to see into the nether reaches of the fabled gardens. In this they were aided by the layout of the villa, which was so simple and open that with all the *shōji* drawn back it was possible to obtain an almost uninterrupted view of the pond, the islands, and the outbuildings that encircled the main residence.

The distractions of Katsura's gardens often led visitors to ignore the appointments of the house, and it was a rare guest who noticed that the house was set precisely nineteen degrees off the traditional north-south axis — to maximize its exposure to winter sunlight while minimizing the effects of summer heat. It is, however, re-

finements of precisely that sort that distinguish the design of the villa, which achieves its effect through accumulated detail rather than initial impact. In the music room of Tomotada's palace, for example, door-pulls take the form of seasonal flower arrangements — cherry blossoms and wisteria for spring, Japanese pampas grass and hibiscus for summer. A less demanding architect than Enshū might have entrusted such a relatively minor task to a local cabinetmaker. Instead, he chose the great Kanō Tanyū, whose works embellish the great reception rooms of Nijo Castle.

This same meticulous sensibility pervades the gardens as well. There a team of twenty-five master gardeners and their assistants labored year round to keep the grounds in a state of perfect readiness for the owners' infrequent visits. Convinced that regular sojourns would spoil their appreciation of the villa's beauties, the family carefully curtailed its excursions, which rarely exceeded one per season. Boating on the villa's artificial lake was confined to the harvest season, which was also the only occasion when the family and their guests remained in the house overnight.

The preservation of Katsura Palace, a task assumed by the imperial household a century ago, requires a rare degree of conscientiousness, for the villa is one of the frailest and most perishable of the world's architectural treasures. Left untended for but a score of years, Katsura would be reduced to rotting fiber and weatherworn beams. Its roofs are bamboo, secured by bamboo nails; they must be replaced every twenty years. Bamboo walls, being less dense, last only fifteen years — which is still five years longer than the tatami mats that cover the villa's floors. The rice-paper *shōji*

that partition the interior must be replaced in six-year cycles, and within that time the mosses that line the garden walkways, trod upon by thousands of tourists, must be replanted three times over.

In sharp contrast, Shūgaku-in Rikyū, the retirement villa of Go-Mizunoo, is almost enhanced by neglect. Its natural setting is spectacular, and it effectively appropriates the blue-green hills north of Kyoto to complete that vista. Sprawling where Katsura is compact, and unpruned where Katsura is manicured, Shūgaku-in overawes initially and occasionally disappoints upon closer inspection. Funds for the construction of this detached palace came from the usual source — the shogunate — but for a rather unusual reason. From the time of his accession, Go-Mizunoo had proved a conspicuously spirited and independent-minded sovereign, and the shogunate, determined to demonstrate its omnipotence, had retaliated by subjecting him to a succession of petty annoyances. In 1619 they compelled him to take a Tokugawa consort, and it soon became clear that the Go-Mizunoo's retirement waited only the arrival of an heir of Tokugawa lineage. To thwart this scheme, the emperor abruptly resigned the throne in 1629 in favor of an eight-year-old daughter — who thus became the first empress-regnant in more than eight centuries, and the first in Kyoto's history.

Dramatic as Emperor Go-Mizunoo's abdication was, its net effect was to place a tractable child on Japan's throne, eliminating the friction between shogunate and crown. The Tokugawa immediately adopted a conciliatory attitude toward their onetime antagonist, and henceforth Go-Mizunoo received a liberal annual stipend from Iemitsu. As early as 1641, the ex-emperor was being officially encouraged to select a site for his retirement villa, and on April 19, 1655, the shogun himself chose the region of Shūgaku-in at the foot of Mount Hiei for that purpose. Several small streams that gushed down the sides of Hiei were backed up behind a great retaining wall of earth and stone to form a broad pond, and work then began on the villa. Go-Mizunoo visited the site as construction progressed, and he apparently liked what he saw. The buildings at Shūgaku-in, whose exteriors were unadorned save for name tablets inscribed in Go-Mizunoo's own hand, declared to all who saw them that the emperor's contemplative life was totally antithetical to the shogun's — and much to be preferred. There can be little question about the emperor's preference, for over the next twenty-five years he returned to the completed villa more than seventy times.

Under Iemitsu, Go-Mizunoo's patron, Japan's feudal institutions were to reach their most refined state. Like the streets of Edo, the Tokugawa bureaucracy seemed to have taken shape in response to the perceived needs of the moment rather than some comprehensive plan. It was Iemitsu who gave this amorphous and inefficient structure its final definition and, in the process, established a mode of government that was to prove both deeply flawed and remarkably durable. It was evident almost from the first that Iemitsu's feudal bureaucracy was unworkable, for it assumed — in complete variance with the facts — that Japan could and would remain a closed agricultural community capable of supporting a large and essentially idle military class. In truth, Japan was beginning to move into a period of unprecedented commercial growth, one that the shogunate lacked the imagination to perceive and the expertise to exploit. Indeed, the Tokugawa scarcely recognized the right to existence of the merchant class, which was defined as parasitical by official ideology, reviled in official proclamations, and discriminated against in official edicts. According to Tokugawa law, all offenses were to be punished "in accordance with social status" — which meant that samurai enjoyed the unquestioned right to slay peasants who offended them, while merchants could be jailed for pressing their samurai debtors.

The result of this policy was the creation of two distinct cultures: the attenuated, nostalgic culture of the samurai, who patronized Nō performances and encouraged the revival of ancient musical forms; and the heady, robust culture of Japan's ascendant merchant class. The former was led by Ieyasu, who stimulated renewed interest in Nō by inviting the nation's four leading dramatic schools to perform in his Kyoto palace. The shogun's enthusiasm was shared by many of his successors, several of whom actually performed in Nō plays staged in the ancient capital.

The artist Ogata Kōrin, who has been labeled the foremost exponent of the courtly arts of seventeenth-century Kyoto, was himself descended from samurai, although his works also reflect the culture of the prosperous merchant class into which his immediate ancestors had married. Until the turn of the century Kyoto and, to a lesser degree, Osaka were the wellsprings of a new cultural movement that reflected the tastes and enthusiasms of the emerging merchant class. Kōrin so totally embodied the spirit of this age that it has been said that his creations "did more than the work of any other artist to arouse the western world to an interest in Japanese art." In 1701, however, an incident occurred that cut short Kōrin's career and presaged the demise of Kyoto as the cultural capital of the nation.

The artist's downfall was precipitated by his decision to attend a picnic in Arashiyama, a mountainous region west of the city. This gathering was in fact little more than an excuse for each of the guests to display his most elegant lacquer and ceramic wares. Eschewing such obvious forms of ostentation, Kōrin produced food wrapped in bamboo leaves — upon which he had executed overall designs in gold. As he finished each course, the artist tossed the gilded fronds into a nearby river. This extraordinary exhibition contravened a three-year-old law prohibiting commoners from using gold or silver, and it led to Kōrin's banishment.

Edo, the city in which Kōrin eventually resettled, was soon to become the center of a vital new urban culture that owed very little to the courtly arts. This new cultural style arose in the "gay quarters," the entertainment districts of Japan's major cities. These enclaves of diversion, which included Gion in Kyoto, Shimmachi in Osaka, and Yoshiwara in Edo, were known as *fuyajō*, or "nightless cities," for their shops never closed and their inhabitants never seemed to sleep. There white-faced geisha performed on the samisen for prosperous merchants, bath girls arranged hasty assignations with perfunctorily disguised samurai, Kabuki theater troupes captivated growing coteries of enthusiasts, and professional raconteurs and jesters roamed the narrow, lantern-hung streets — all in a "floating world" of carnal pleasure and carnival color.

From this "floating world" came a style of painting known as *ukiyo-e,* which, being a reflection of plebeian

Edo, the administrative capital of the Tokugawa regime, was to become the hub of a new urban culture that reflected the carnival atmosphere of the city's brothel district rather than the refined, nostalgic atmosphere of the imperial court. The prosperous merchants who visited Edo's "gay quarter" referred to it as ukiyo — *"the floating world." In time, that phrase was also applied to the new medium used to celebrate that milieu, the wood-block print. Willowy, heavily powdered geisha such as those pictured at left were a favorite subject of* ukiyo-e *printmakers, but leading actors of the Kabuki theater were also featured (lower left). The actor's portrait at right, credited to Tōshūsai Sharaku, is one of 145 that the artist created in a ten-month period in 1794–95.*

tastes, was scorned by the upper classes. It was anything but unrefined, however, and its foremost product, the wood-block print, was to reintroduce the Orient to the Occident in the eighteenth century. The art of block printing had been known in Japan since the eighth century, but its enormous popularity and widespread dissemination date from the seventeenth, when wood-block designs were first added to printed pamphlets and books. Hishikawa Moronobu, the founder of the school of *ukiyo-e*, worked only in monochrome and focused exclusively on life in Edo's entertainment quarter, but his successors recognized no such technical and thematic restraints. Around 1760, for instance, Suzuki Harunobu began experimenting with the use of multiple-block printing, a Chinese refinement introduced through Nagasaki that permitted the introduction of color and halftones. Heretofore, *ukiyo-e* prints had been handcolored, a process that lacked both the subtlety and the consistency of color printing. From this point on, wood-block printing would be a collaboration between the painter, who designed the print; the woodcutter, who executed it; the printer, who made the definitive selection of colors; and the publisher, who distributed the finished product.

Harunobu's other major contribution to the advancement of *ukiyo-e* technique lay in extending the artistic horizons of the movement beyond the confines of the entertainment quarter. His notable contemporary, Torii Kiyonaga, whom many consider the greatest of all *ukiyo-e* artists, was to focus almost exclusively on female subjects, but he refused to restrict himself to the women of Yoshiwara. Kiyonaga, scion of a family noted for its Kabuki theater billboards, devoted print after

Plagued by official censorship, many of Japan's leading eighteenth-century writers abandoned the scandal-ridden world of the Kabuki theater and wrote instead for the sophisticated form of puppet theater shown in this contemporary painting. At Bunraku performances, both music and dialogue were supplied by players seated upon an elevated dais (far right), while puppeteers manipulated the "actors" onstage.

print to women of all walks of life, finding in each the same elegant, ethereal quality, the same mysterious distancing. In time his gorgeously costumed, physiologically anonymous women were to become the symbols of a cultural renaissance that included not only painting but poetry, puppetry, and porcelain.

Originally centered in Kyoto and Osaka, this vigorous new cultural force had soon swept east to Edo, which in the century since Sekigahara had become the largest city in the world, with a population in excess of one million. It was during this period that haiku, a short, epigrammatic poetic form of surprising versatility, was popularized by Matsuo Bashō and his followers. Equally popular were the novels of Ihara Saikaku, an Osaka merchant whose tales of the "floating world" include such randy works as *The Man Who Spent His Life at Love-making* and the equally titillating *The Woman Who Loved Love.*

Parallel advances in the world of the theater — encouraged by rising popular enthusiasm for Kabuki, which is sometimes identified as "the poor man's Nō" — produced Chikamatsu Monzaemon, the Shakespeare of Japan. It is intriguing to note that Monzaemon's considerable reputation is based almost exclusively upon works for Bunraku, or puppet theater, rather than Kabuki, although he wrote prolifically for both. By Monzaemon's time the rampant amorality of Kabuki players had become something of a permanent affront to what the shogunate perceived to be the public's sense of decency. Consequently, women had been banned from Kabuki companies and plays were regularly suppressed by government censors. Such restrictions did not apply to puppet theater, of course, and for thirty

years Monzaemon wrote chiefly for this elegant, refined, and altogether serious dramatic medium.

Chikamatsu Monzaemon's dramas, which depended heavily upon recitative and incident, commonly treated the theme of thwarted love culminating in a suicide pact. In general, they reflected the strictest principles of contemporary neo-Confucian ethics. The same cannot be said for the era's most famous collaboration, *Chūshingura,* the saga of the forty-seven masterless samurai whose dedication to the ancient concept of *bushidō,* the way of the warrior, has enthralled generations of theatergoers. The historic incident upon which three of Monzaemon's contemporaries based their drama occurred in Edo in April, 1701. Lord Asano, a virtuous provincial daimyo, had come to the capital to rehearse his role in a forthcoming state ceremony. Ignorant of court etiquette and eager to avoid any embarrassment to his clan, Asano sought instruction from Lord Kira, a venal and corrupt member of the shogun's inner circle who demanded a substantial bribe in exchange for his services. Asano's steadfast refusal to capitulate to Kira's demands precipitated a confrontation in which the former superficially wounded the latter. Tokugawa house law expressly prohibited the drawing of swords in the shogun's palace, and when Asano refused to defend his actions his examiners had no choice but to order him to commit *seppuku.*

With the death of their master and the confiscation of his fief, the samurai serving the Asano household became *rōnin,* masterless men-at-arms. For almost two years they led lives of conspicuous dissolution designed to convince Kira's spies that they had been utterly demoralized by their master's death. Throughout this

period they secretly plotted their revenge, and on January 30, 1703, these loyal warriors forced their way into Kira's Edo mansion, slew the man who had wrought their downfall, and surrendered to the authorities. The *rōnin* fully expected to die for their actions, and they were consequently taken aback by the ensuing debate over their fate. The shogun was eager to pardon them, but his closest advisers, who placed pragmatic considerations above *bushidō* ideals, insisted that the warriors must die. After two months' delay, the surviving *rōnin* were ordered to commit suicide.

The plight of Lord Asano's retainers, whose actions were admirable according to samurai ideology but culpable in the eyes of the Tokugawa bureaucracy, illustrates the degree to which economic and political conditions had combined, by 1700, to humble this once-mighty caste. Conversion to hard currency — an inevitability in Iemitsu's day and an accomplished fact by the first decade of the eighteenth century — had proved disastrous for samurai and daimyo alike. Their incomes, traditionally measured in terms of bushels of rice and consequently pegged to the price of grain, fluctuated wildly from year to year. A *koku* of rice, worth 230 units of silver in 1715, was worth only 35 units three years later. Frequent currency debasements and government-imposed austerity programs — the shogunate's only means of coping with the unstable and unpredictable commodities market — compounded the nobles' agonies. By the time of Iemitsu's death in 1651, most feudal houses were able to sustain operations only by borrowing repeatedly and heavily from the merchant class. Rates were usurious and the prospects of repayment dim, for by this time the daimyo owed debts estimated at one hundred times the face value of the coins in circulation in the entire country. The barons' annual interest payments — had they been able to meet them — would have absorbed fully a quarter of all the revenues they generated.

To deal with the nation's ruinously erratic economy, the eighth Tokugawa shogun, Yoshimune, imposed a new round of austerity measures when he assumed office in 1716. After decades of mismanagement or outright neglect, Japan's economy had become ungovernable, and it refused to submit to Yoshimune's stern but unimaginative reforms, which actually sought to restore order by reviving discredited forms of feudal regimentation. The disintegration of the country's economic fabric was hastened by a series of major famines, which occurred at regular intervals throughout the eighteenth and early nineteenth centuries. A million peasants died of starvation during the great famine of 1780–86, and thereafter repeated food shortages produced violent agrarian risings. Even the widespread practice of *mabiki*, or "thinning" — the euphemism for infanticide — failed to stabilize the population.

In Kyoto, economic calamity gave way to civil catastrophe in the spring of 1788. Around midmorning on March sixth of that year, a strong wind sprang up in the east. It gathered force throughout the day, until by nightfall winds of hurricane velocity were buffeting the capital, and men and animals who ventured into the streets were blown over. Early the following morning a fire broke out in a money-changing shop on the right bank of the Kamo River. The populace of the imperiled city turned out in force to combat Kyoto's ancient foe, but to no avail. Driven by the high winds, flames tore

In a sense, Kabuki theater was the floating world in microcosm — by turns frenetic and garish, serene and gorgeous. The magnificently detailed painting at right depicts a Kabuki troupe in the throes of preparation for a performance, from toilette and costuming to make-up and musicians' practice. Although unsigned, this screen is attributed to Hishikawa Moronobu, the father of ukiyo-e.

great holes in the city's wooden core and skipped across its thatched rooftops. For two days the hapless citizens stood by as the conflagration flickered and appeared to die in one quarter — only to flare anew in another. Not until noon on March ninth did the fire burn itself out, and by that time every princely home on either side of the Kamo had been destroyed. The Great Fire of Temmei, as the holocaust has come to be known, had reduced all but the outlying areas of the city to acrid, smouldering debris. Thirty-seven shrines, 909 principal and subsidiary temples, and 183,000 homes had been reduced to dense gray ash by one of the worst fires in world history.

The process of rebuilding began almost immediately, but work was severely hampered by endemic civil unrest and economic instability. By the dawn of the nineteenth century, these internal pressures had built to intolerable levels. There were nineteen currency debasements between 1819 and 1837, and the crop failures of the 1820's produced famines in the north in 1833 and across the nation three years later. At the same time, concerted pressure was being applied from without. China had recently been opened to international trade, and England, France, the Netherlands, Russia, and the United States were all pressuring Japan to end its centuries-old policy of closure and resume its diplomatic and commercial role in East Asia. For decades the shogunate staunchly refused all foreign overtures — and then, in 1853, a squadron of U.S. warships steamed into Edo Bay. The commander of that expeditionary force had come at the behest of his President to insist, in new and bolder language, that Japan open its doors to the West.

VII

City of a Thousand Shrines

The four "black ships" that steamed into Edo Bay in July of 1853 flew the distinctive ensign of the most aggressive new imperialist power in the Pacific — the United States of America. Their presence reflected the determination of an otherwise unprepossessing American President, Millard Fillmore, to succeed where others had failed for half a century — by extracting a limited trade agreement from the insular, obdurate Tokugawa shogunate. To fulfill this ambition, Fillmore had commissioned Commodore Matthew Calbraith Perry, a veteran of forty-four years of naval duty, to hand deliver an official communiqué to "the emperor of the Japanese." The men with whom Perry would actually be dealing, the shogun's inner circle of advisers, had learned of his impending arrival several months before the American squadron was first sighted off Shimoda, a tiny fishing village on the tip of the Izu Peninsula. Nevertheless, the appearance of the heavily armed, smoke-belching American steamships produced a mood of near-panic in Edo and its environs.

Nowhere was that furor more intense than in Edo Castle. A contemporary historian reports that the shogun was "exceedingly troubled, and summoned all the officials to a council" — where it soon became apparent that the shogunate lacked the capacity to repel the foreigners. Unable to perform his ancient office, that of *sei-i tai*, or "barbarian-subduing," the Tokugawa shogun seemed to have no choice but to capitulate to the American commander's demands for an audience. The more pragmatic and worldwise of his advisers counseled such a step, but the daimyo of western Honshu and Kyushu expressed inalterable opposition to any form of accommodation.

While official couriers were conveying the shogun's request to his vassals, Perry dropped anchor off Uraga. Calling himself "admiral" to enhance his image — and consequently his bargaining position — in Japanese eyes, the American commodore reiterated his request for an audience with the "emperor." The shogun's officials, equally adept at diplomatic fencing, responded by sending only minor officials — masquerading as great lords — out to Perry's ships.

The men under Perry's command knew him to be a stern taskmaster, a tireless organizer, and a dynamic leader. They also knew him to be possessed of a sense of dignity that bordered on pomposity — a quality that served the American well in his dealings with the Japanese, who closely associated mien and rank. In the end, of course, the shogun had little choice but to accept President Fillmore's letter, for Perry's ships could at any time have thrown a blockade across the narrow neck of Edo Bay, closing this principal conduit to the city's produce markets and literally starving the Tokugawa shogunate into submission.

Having achieved his initial goal, Perry withdrew to the Ryukyu Islands, off the southern coast of Kyushu, to await the shogun's reply. In a sense, that response never did come, for the incumbent shogun died ten days after Perry's withdrawal, plunging the government into an inescapable round of distracting public ceremonies. In mid-February of the following year, 1854 — earlier than anticipated — Perry returned to Edo Bay. This time his fleet consisted of eight ships — one quarter of the entire American navy — and this time negotiations were conducted at Kanagawa, a step closer to the Tokugawa capital itself.

At Kanagawa the Japanese were to yield, grudgingly, to the inevitability of commercial intercourse with the West. Bowing to Perry's demands — and to the gunboat diplomacy that backed them up — the shogunate agreed to open the ports of Hakodate and Shimoda to Western trade, and to accept the establishment of an American consulate in the latter. Perry's delegation, elated over the concessions they had succeeded in obtaining, were some time in realizing how limited those concessions really were. Hakodate, after all, was located on the largely unsettled northern island of Hokkaido, and Shimoda, although convenient to Pacific sea lanes, lay more than one hundred mountainous miles from Edo.

To mark the signing of the Treaty of Kanagawa, the Japanese staged a *sumō* wrestling bout for their American guests. Perry's party reciprocated with a minstrel show, a gesture that can only have perplexed the shogun's delegates. The inappropriateness of the Americans' choice of entertainment could not diminish the significance of their accomplishment, however. After two centuries of strict isolation, Japan had finally been opened to the West — without the loss of a single life or the appropriation of a single acre of territory.

In the summer of 1856 the United States exercised for the first time its right to appoint a consul to Japan. Fortunately for the course of future relations between the two countries, the man chosen for that post, Townsend Harris, was able to rise above the petty humiliations that greeted him upon his arrival in Shimoda. Indeed, Harris's rare diplomatic skills, extraordinary perseverance, and engaging personality were to win for the United States what no foreign representative had ever succeeded in securing — a full trade agreement with Tokugawa Japan. The Russians, beginning in 1792 with an envoy named Laxman who established contact with the shogunate through Hakodate, had been pressing their suit for six decades — and the English had for nearly as long. Vessels chartered by the British East India Company had first entered Japan's coastal waters in 1797, and late that same year the *Eliza,* a Dutch ship sailing under American flag, had also put into Nagasaki harbor. Thereafter at regular intervals the maritime powers of the West had sought to negotiate some sort of basic accord with the Japanese. Short of a trade agreement, each hoped at least to obtain permission to put into Japanese ports in foul weather, and there to take on fresh water and provisions. With the advent of steam, the need for coaling stations also became a pressing consideration.

Japan lay along the great circle route from the Pacific coast of the United States to China, a sea lane regularly plied by American merchantmen, who consequently had the greatest stake in achieving an accord with the Tokugawa. A diplomatic offensive was joined in earnest in 1837, when a Canton-based American businessman sent one of his own ships to Edo to repatriate seven Japanese castaways. The response to this gesture was immediate and unambiguous: as the unarmed ship steamed up Edo Bay, the gun emplacements at Uraga opened fire upon her.

The Americans were not to be dissuaded, however, and in 1846 another American delegation put into Edo Bay to press for negotiations. This time the guns of Uraga lay silent; cooler heads had prevailed in the highest Tokugawa councils, and the shogun had agreed to pro forma consideration of the American appeal.

Proponents of "Dutch Learning" — as the study of Western technology, filtered through the Dutch trading post at Nagasaki, was called — had convinced the nation's leaders that inflexible opposition to the Western powers was foolhardy. It remained for those leaders to convince the emperor in Kyoto and the intensely xenophobic daimyo of western Honshu and Kyushu.

This latter task was to prove nearly impossible, for it called upon a military dictatorship that had governed for centuries by fiat to resolve its greatest dilemma by consensus. One reason the Tokugawa found themselves in this quandary was that the administrative system of 1854 bore little resemblance to the compact feudal bureaucracy of Iemitsu's day. In the intervening centuries the power of the shogunate had steadily eroded, until control of the country lay in the hands of an inner circle of Tokugawa daimyo who administered a cumbersome and inefficient shogunal bureaucracy. It was these daimyo who met in Edo Castle in February, 1854, to consider Perry's petition for an audience with the "emperor." And it was these daimyo, unable to reconcile the demands of the nation and the harsher realities of gunboat diplomacy, who permitted the government to sink into a state of administrative paralysis. In Confucian terms, the Tokugawa had lost their mandate to govern — and in the opinion of many, that mantle had passed to the emperor himself. In the future, imperial sanction would be sought on virtually all issues of national consequence.

In this atmosphere of confusion and indirection, Townsend Harris was able to negotiate a landmark agreement between the United States and Japan in 1858. Arguing that a full trade agreement with the Americans was preferable to a less favorable treaty with any other Western power, Harris convinced the shogunate to open Yokohama and Nagasaki to unrestricted American trade. The provisions of the new treaty met with vigorous opposition in Kyoto, which had once again become the focus of internal political affairs, and the Tokugawa soon regretted having sought the emperor's imprimatur on their highly unpopular dealings with the United States. The Harris treaty was followed in close order by a spate of others — with England, Russia, France, and the Netherlands — and these serial concessions to the Western powers deeply divided the ruling clique. Worse still, Shogun Iesada died without heir shortly after the Harris treaty was signed.

For leadership in this time of national crisis the daimyo turned to Ii Naosuke, a pragmatist committed to reestablishing the shogunate's authority, who took command of the government under the title of *tairō*, or "great councillor." In a move aimed at assuring the success of his policy of rapprochement with the West, the *tairō* initiated a systematic purge of all opponents of his views, a brutal scheme that led to Naosuke's assassination in 1860. In a very real sense the shogunate died with the great councillor, for thereafter no Tokugawa leader was able to rise above the factionalism that consumed the shogunate or control the opposition that swept the country.

The years immediately following Naosuke's assassination were marked by administrative ataxia, increasing dependence upon imperial sanction, and terrorist attacks upon foreign nationals. By 1863, the Tokugawa mandate was in tatters. The government was unable to prevent bands of samurai from attacking British,

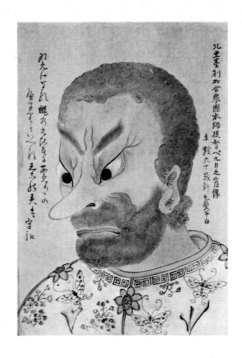

Although it professes to be "a True Portrait of Perry, Envoy of the Republic of North America," the hirsute and demonic countenance at right is actually a composite portrait of a foreigner as interpreted by a native artist shortly after the opening of Japan. The events that surrounded Commodore Perry's arrival in 1853 are the subject of the contemporary woodcut seen below. Its outer panels, grouped around a fanciful map of the world, depict (clockwise from the upper right): the landing at Uraga, an American warship at anchor, Perry's men on parade, a group of samurai in battle dress, and the sumō wrestling contest that concluded the Americans' visit.

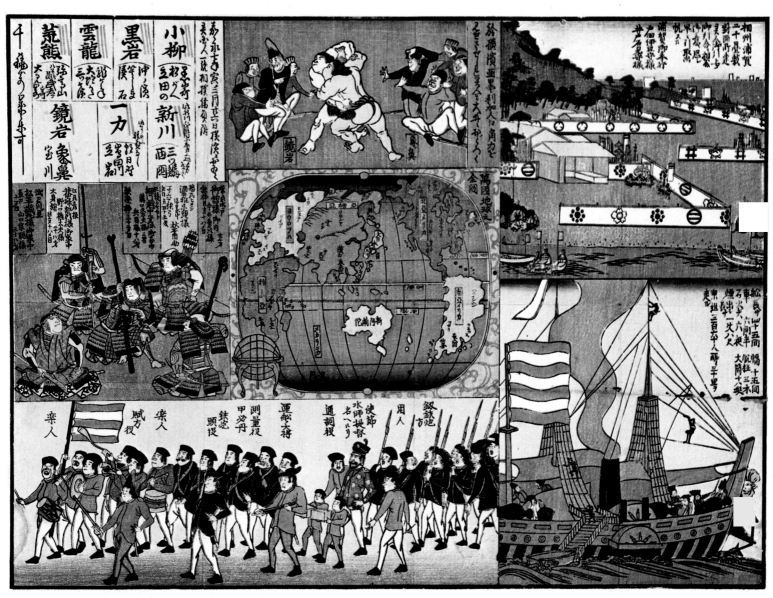

Dutch, and American citizens at will — nor could it prevent the Western powers from bombarding Japanese cities in retaliation. And when the emperor summoned the shogun to Kyoto to explain these outrages, the titular leader of the Tokugawa had no choice but to comply. On this journey, Shogun Iemochi was accompanied by roughly three thousand retainers. Tokugawa Iemitsu, making the same trip for very different reasons 230 years earlier, is said to have been escorted by an army of 300,000.

The Tokugawa era, which had begun with the triumph of Sekigahara, was to end in a series of burning humiliations, not the least of which was a Western attack upon a Honshu port that forced a new and far more comprehensive treaty upon the emperor. Two years later, a brace of closely related events was to bring the era to its unhappy close. First, the conservative emperor Kōmei, a long-time supporter of isolationist elements in the government, died and was succeeded by his fourteen-year-old son, Mutsuhito. At the same time, Tokugawa Yoshinobu assumed the office of shogun amid widespread agitation for the restoration of imperial government. Yoshinobu, who approached the shogunate with reluctance but executed his office with commendable vigor, was convinced of the necessity of reform, and he labored tirelessly in Kyoto to salvage some role for the shogunate in the years to come.

By November of 1867, it had become clear that the shogun's political position was no longer tenable, and Yoshinobu offered to resign in favor of the emperor, turning over the administration of the nation to a council of great daimyo headed by a member of the Tokugawa clan. These concessions, however, were insufficient in the eyes of the activists of the Kyoto court and their anti-Tokugawa allies, who abolished the shogunate altogether in January, 1868, and excluded the Tokugawa from any further participation in the government. A brief, lackluster civil war followed, in the course of which Tokugawa forces attempted to seize Kyoto but were easily repelled after a brief skirmish near the site of Fushimi Castle. Shortly thereafter, an imperial army marched on Edo, where Tokugawa forces surrendered without a fight.

The first year of the new emperor's reign marked the beginning of a new epoch in Japanese history, one known as the *Meiji Jidai* or Era of Enlightened Rule, and consequently Mutsuhito is known as the Meiji Emperor. The people of Japan saw Mutsuhito as an energetic and progressive leader — the very wellspring of the nation's modern history — but in truth he was little more than a figurehead; political power belonged to the samurai who had engineered the restoration of imperial rule.

During the first critical years of the Meiji period Japan was favored with a large number of extremely able leaders. These men were by and large young — their average age in 1868 was only thirty. They were for the most part the sons of lower-level samurai, but some had enjoyed special educational opportunities, including travel abroad. They were, therefore, unfettered by the preconceptions and prejudices common to their older, more insular colleagues, and as a result they were able to achieve a number of long-overdue reforms in a remarkably short space of time.

The first of these reforms was an about-face on foreign policy, signaled in March, 1868, by the Meiji

Emperor's decision to receive representatives of the Western powers in Kyoto. He did so at the behest of his samurai advisers, who could think of no clearer expression of Japan's desire for detente with the West, and he did so in the recently rebuilt Imperial Palace. But it had become clear to the men who now guided Japan's destiny that Edo had served as the true administrative center of the nation for so long that it would be impractical to abandon that city in favor of the old imperial capital. Instead, it was decided to move the emperor and his retinue to Edo. On September 3, 1868, the former Tokugawa stronghold was renamed Tokyo, "Eastern Capital," and in May of the following year Mutsuhito moved into the refurbished shogunal palace. Kyoto, which had been the seat of imperial power for 1,075 years, would henceforth serve the imperial family only as a stage for coronations.

The leaders of the restoration — a group that included descendants of the illustrious Fujiwara such as Saionji Kimmochi — next turned their attention to the task of dismantling Japan's anachronistic feudal system. Like the Taika Reform of 645–50, this attempt to alter the nation's power structure achieved its objectives without recourse to violence. In the main, this was possible because of the resiliency and adaptability of the civil administration, which was still capable of providing the country with effective local government. In part, of course, fear of invasion also encouraged conciliation during the early years of the restoration. The Japanese had before them the unsettling example of Manchu China, which the Western powers had recently divided into lucrative trading spheres.

Determined to avoid such blatant exploitation, the leaders of Meiji Japan moved rapidly to abolish the feudal system. In 1869, the daimyo of western Japan who had played prominent parts in the imperial restoration were persuaded to take the lead in formally ceding their domains to the emperor in exchange for annual pensions. Once this was done, the other daimyo were morally obliged to follow suit. Two years later the government officially abolished all daimyo fiefs, erased all daimyo debts, and established a handsome program of pensions for the now-landless barons. The next step was to disband the nation's enormous, idle samurai class. This reform was also achieved in several stages, beginning with the introduction of universal conscription in 1872. For members of Japan's hereditary warrior caste, this meant an immediate and devastating loss of status — and an eventual and concomitant loss of income.

The speed with which these reforms were achieved stunned the West, which had been inclined to dismiss the Japanese as the barbarians of the Orient, incapable of entering the comity of nations. To their astonishment, Meiji Japan was to evolve into a world military power in the space of a few decades through a program of rapid Westernization and systematic modernization. Both these forces were at work during the first years of the Meiji era, but the former reached its apogee in the 1880's and began to decline just as the latter was beginning to exert a telling influence on national life.

In Japanese history, indiscriminate assimilation has always preceded adaptation and innovation, and so it was in the decades immediately following the signing of the Harris treaty, as the Japanese hastened to adopt Western dress, manners, cuisine, hair styles, patent

medicines, and dentifrices. In some cases this form of voguish ostentation was carred to ridiculous extremes: oppressive, sunless Victorian parlors were appended to traditional Japanese houses, kimono-clad merchants took to wearing top hats and carrying Malacca canes, and graceless, uninspired red-brick buildings were erected along the Ginza, Tokyo's principal boulevard. The cumulative effect of these excesses was to create antipathy toward further superficial Westernization, leading to a turn-of-the-century reemphasis on traditional modes of dress and deportment.

Modernization, a concurrent phenomenon of the latter half of the nineteenth century, was to have a far more significant material impact upon Japanese life. The Meiji government, which alone was capable, in the years following the collapse of the Tokuwaga regime, of marshalling the manpower and revenues necessary to achieve broad-ranging technological reform, initiated many of these changes. In the 1850's, for instance, internal transportation was so primitive that it cost as much to move a ton of goods fifty miles inland as it had cost to ship those same goods all the way from Europe. The famed Tōkaidō, the highway linking Tokyo and Kyoto, was adequate to accommodate sedan chairs, imperial couriers, and market-bound merchants, but inadequate to handle the tons of commercial goods now pouring into Japan's port cities. To facilitate the distribution of this merchandise, the government began constructing a national railway system. The first branch, which linked the former fishing village of Yokohama to the new capital of Tokyo in 1872, was to prove immensely profitable. The revenues it generated and the example it set encouraged the laying of more track on a speculative basis, and by 1877 Kyoto had been linked to the growing network of rails.

The last decades of the nineteenth century were also years of remarkable international initiatives, none more astonishing, in Western eyes, than the opening of Korea in 1874. Little more than a score of years after Perry first showed the American flag in Edo Bay, the Japanese used precisely the same sort of gunboat diplomacy to coerce the Koreans into signing a special trade agreement that ultimately led to complete control of the peninsula. Seized by imperialistic fervor, the leaders of Meiji Japan next embarked upon the conquest of China. The Sino-Japanese War of 1894–95, which marked Japan's coming of age as an imperial power, demonstrated a clear mastery of modern military technology. The Manchus, who sued for peace almost immediately, were obliged to cede Taiwan, the neighboring Pescadores Islands, and the Liaotung Peninsula in southern Manchuria to the Japanese.

Emboldened by their effortless victory over the Chinese, the Japanese waited less than a decade before setting upon their other major rival in northern China, imperial Russia. Establishing an ominous military precedent, the Meiji emperor's forces first destroyed the Russian fleet at Port Arthur, on the Liaotung Peninsula, and then declared war on the Romanov empire. The Russians, although deemed militarily superior to the Japanese, were compelled to sustain their campaign at the terminus of a single railroad track that was thousands of miles long. As a result they were never able to mount a decisive counterattack, and after less than two years of bitter and inconclusive warfare both sides welcomed President Theodore

Roosevelt's offer to mediate a settlement. That treaty, which was signed at Portsmouth, New Hampshire, on September 5, 1905, restored Manchuria to the Chinese but reasserted Japan's claim to Liaotung. More significantly, it recognized that for the first time in modern history an Asian nation had bested Europeans in a war. The death of the Meiji Emperor seven years later brought the first phase of Japan's modern growth to a close. The foundation of the new imperial state had been laid; the ensuing decades would witness the growth of a dynamic world empire.

World War I, which decimated the male population, ravaged the countryside, and severely strained the economy of Western Europe, spelled the end of unconstrained imperialism in the West. Japan suffered no such depredations, and as a result it was alone among the nations that gathered at Versailles in 1919 in lacking any incentive to abandon imperialistic policies. In point of fact, Japan had compelling reasons for actively pursuing an expansionist policy, for by the 1920's the country was growing too rapidly to be contained. The population, which had leveled off at 30 million during the famine-ridden eighteenth century, had jumped to 55 million by 1900, and in the same period Tokyo's population had topped 2 million, nearly doubling. Japan's acute shortage of arable land and natural resources had made it dependent upon imported food-stuffs and raw materials, and this, coupled with a need for new foreign markets, had led it to adopt a policy of voracious imperialism.

The relationship with China had become particularly delicate by 1920, for Japan was by then importing nearly all of its coal, pig iron, and cotton fiber from the mainland. Fiber converted into bolts of cloth constituted Japan's prime export — and half of those bolts were sold back to China. Both businessmen and military leaders recognized the high risks inherent in such a relationship, which could be jeopardized by the slightest rift between the Asian powers or any of their Western allies. To prevent such a development, the Japanese government pursued a public policy of complete cooperation with the West while simultaneously advancing its private scheme to build an empire in the Pacific. Thus, in 1920 Japan joined the League of Nations; in 1928 it signed the Kellogg-Briand Pact renouncing war; and in 1930, in the face of vehement popular opposition, it ratified the London Naval Treaty, which pegged the growth of the Japanese navy to that of Great Britain and the United States, perpetuating the Western powers' position of superiority.

The 1930 treaty marked the highwater mark of Japanese cooperation with the Western powers. A year later, in September, 1931, the unalloyed imperialistic ambitions of the men who dominated Japanese politics were laid bare in an extraordinary military action that the Japanese themselves would euphemistically label "the Manchurian Incident." In a lightning campaign that was to prove a turning point in the nation's modern history, an imperial army overran southern Manchuria, established the puppet state of Manchukuo, and embarked upon an elaborate empirical test of modern economic development. The speed with which Manchukuo became economically self-sufficient graphically demonstrated the ability of the army, acting in concert with the nation's great industrial monopolies, or *zaibatsu,* to rapidly develop large overseas territories. So effective was this prototypical military-industrial complex that within five years Japan had doubled its exports, becoming, in the process, the first major power to recover from the effects of the Great Depression.

In Japan, the 1930's were years of rampant nationalism, much of it focused on the emperor, whom followers of the revitalized state cult of Shinto had come to regard as divine. They were also years of ascendant militarism, secret ultranationalist societies with names like Blood Brotherhood and Heavenly Sword Party, and politics by assassination. Between May of 1932 and February of 1936 these clandestine societies killed premiers, cabinet officers, industrialists, and influential private citizens alike in an effort to bring down the government and reshape the nation's foreign policy. Then, in 1937, an incident occurred that was to achieve in a few months what terrorist attacks had failed to achieve in four sanguinary years — Japan's total involvement in a quest for empire. In July of that year, an inconsequential skirmish between Chinese and Japanese troops on the outskirts of Peking had suddenly erupted into full-scale war. The Imperial Army, which anticipated a victory as swift as the one gained in Manchuria in 1931, instead found itself embroiled in a seemingly ceaseless campaign against an elusive enemy.

Trapped in an amorphous, shifting, inconclusive guerrilla war, the Japanese imperial offensive suffered its first major setback. The cost of maintaining an army of occupation in China exceeded $4,000,000 a day, and the cost in terms of national prestige was intolerable. "Caught in a situation in which only victory would satisfy the national honor," Edwin O. Reischauer observes, "the Japanese bled themselves in a cause in which simple military victory was essentially impossible." By 1940, the nation's heavily propagandized "holy war" against the Chinese had led to full mobilization and to military domination of all aspects of domestic life — what Prince Konoe, the acting premier, called an "advanced national defense state." By the fall of 1940, when the Japanese signed a treaty with the Axis powers, Paris had fallen and the way was clear for the Japanese to move unopposed into French Indochina, the vital center of Western interests in Asia.

America, Britain, and China — joined by the Dutch in what was known as the ABCD Embargo — responded to the Japanese offensive in Indochina by cutting off shipping with the home islands. With oil imports reduced by 90 per cent, the Japanese high command faced the prospect of a critical fuel shortage, one that would hamper all phases of its Pacific operations. And when negotiations to lift the embargo collapsed in September of 1941, the nation's highest council adopted a resolution calling for war against the United States if no diplomatic solution to Japan's dilemma could be found. This resolution was accepted with scant enthusiasm by Emperor Hirohito, who chose the occasion to read a poem written years earlier by his grandfather, the Meiji Emperor:

> Since all are brothers in the world,
> Why is there such constant turmoil?

The prospect of war with the United States, onerous as it was, struck many Japanese as preferable to retreat from China, an action that might have provoked civil insurrection at home. In addition, the Americans were thought to lack both the resolve and the capacity to sustain a protracted war in the Pacific. This miscalcula-

tion was to prove fatal, for the aerial attack on the U.S. naval installation at Pearl Harbor, far from forcing the United States to rescind the ABCD Embargo, only galvanized the American war effort.

It took time for the United States to achieve full wartime production, however, and for the first year of the war Japan's imperial juggernaut leveled all before it. In short order the Philippines, Hong Kong, Singapore, and Indonesia fell, and by March of 1942 the Japanese army was in New Guinea — poised for an attack upon Australia — and in Burma, ready to strike at the subcontinent of India. Then, in June of that year, the Imperial Navy lost four of its first-line aircraft carriers at Midway, and two months later the Allies landed at Guadalcanal, launching the first phase of an island-hopping counterattack. The Gilbert Islands were retaken, then the Marshalls, and finally the Philippines. American submarines annihilated the Japanese merchant navy, and in the second half of 1944 the systematic fire bombing of the home islands began. In all, 668,000 civilians died in those raids — more than 100,-000 of them in a single, massive incendiary attack on Tokyo. Still the high command refused to countenance surrender — and so, on August 6, a new type of bomb slid from the belly of a B-29 as it passed high over Hiroshima. Three days later, a second atomic bomb obliterated the port of Nagasaki — the city of the Christian martyrs, the seat of "Dutch Learning," the Tokugawa "keyhole on the world." In the face of these twin holocausts, the emperor was compelled to "endure the unendurable." Japan would surrender, unconditionally, to its first foreign conqueror.

It had been widely — and erroneously — reported that Kyoto was to be the target of a third American A-bomb, should the government refuse to capitulate. Japan's surrender on August 15 obviated all such speculation, but the truth was that the decision had been made to spare Kyoto. As late as January of 1945, Kyoto had been listed for destruction by the head of the U.S. armed forces in the Pacific, who argued that the former imperial capital was an important manufacturing center with a population of 753,000, and consequently a priority target. But his decision was reversed shortly thereafter by Secretary of War Henry L. Stimson, who later commented: "I struck off the list of suggested targets the city of Kyoto. Although it was a target of considerable military importance, it had been the ancient capital of Japan and was a shrine of Japanese art and culture."

As a result of Stimson's decision, Kyoto was spared all but occasional accidental strafings. Like the ancient German university city of Heidelberg, Kyoto was to survive the war virtually unscathed. Incidental bombings destroyed ninety-one houses during the war years and claimed eighty-two lives, but it was the citizens of Kyoto themselves who most altered the face of the city, pulling down 19,806 additional houses to create firebreaks in the oldest quarters.

During the height of the conflict weavers and dyers from Kyoto were drafted to work in the great munitions factories in Kobe and Osaka, where they labored side-by-side with craftsmen who had formerly produced Kyoto's renowned lacquerware and cloisonné. On the outskirts of the former capital new factories were constructed to produce electrical appliances, parachute cords, and radio tubes. Mitsubishi, one of the na-

During the final months of World War II, brutally efficient firebombing leveled much of Tokyo (left); during the final days, atomic bombs obliterated Hiroshima and the ancient port of Nagasaki. Kyoto, recognized as "a shrine of Japanese art and culture," was spared. Its great temples and sprawling palaces survived the war virtually unscathed, pockets of order in the midst of chaos. Only with the revival of the nation's economy did groups of pilgrims begin to return in numbers to such favored prewar sites as the viewing platform of Kiyomizu-dera (below).

tion's largest *zaibatsu,* opened two aircraft assembly plants in the suburbs. As Kyoto became increasingly involved in the war effort, industrial employment rose from a prewar high of 80,000 to almost 120,000. At the same time, however, employment in the city's textile center — which traced its name, Nishijin, or "Western Camp," back to the days of the Onin War — fell from 23,000 to less than 4,000.

Five days after Hirohito accepted the Allies' surrender terms, Kyoto's civic leaders voted to convert the new factories on the city's periphery to the production of farming implements and cooking utensils. And during the first year of the Allied occupation, when such costly commodities as gold dust and raw silk were unavailable to local artisans, it was these prosaic industries that supported the city's economy. Gold dust, vital to the production of decorated lacquerware, and raw silk, from which Kyoto's internationally famous brocades were woven, were released only to manufacturers who were willing to produce their wares exclusively for export to the United States. With the domestic market in total disarray, Kyoto's artisans had little choice but to comply, despite the fact that competition for this restricted foreign market forced unwelcome reductions in the quality of goods produced.

As a result, Kyoto's postwar recovery lagged somewhat behind that of the great manufacturing centers, and for a time it appeared that she might never fully recover. As late as 1958 a Western journalist described the city as "a great, rotting capital city left over from another age and dying slowly on the flat floor of a wide valley." The obituary was premature, however. Stimson had rightly called Kyoto a "shrine of Japanese

*The lines were written about Kinkaku-ji, the famed
Golden Pavilion, but they may fairly be applied to
countless other sites in and around Japan's ancient
imperial capital. Indeed, they speak for all of Kyoto
— in any age, in any season:*

> *The mountain is sharply etched,*
>   *the woods are colorful,*
>   *the valleys deep, streams rapid.*
> *Moonlight is clear on a softly*
>   *breathing wind.*
> *Man reads in the quietness*
>   *scripture without words.*

art and culture," and her renascence waited only the recovery of Japan's battered economy. As the nation prospered, its citizens resumed their pilgrimages to the "city of a thousand shrines," coming in small groups each spring to view the cherry blossoms.

By 1961 that trickle of tourists had become a torrent, with almost 18 million visitors a year streaming through the ancient imperial capital. A decade later the annual total topped 33 million, only 300,000 of whom were foreigners. With nearly one quarter of the population of Japan passing through the city each year, Kyoto's tourist bonanza has become a civic burden. The exhaust fumes of tourist buses and private cars compounds the city's already serious air-pollution problem, corroding the metal fittings of scores of national monuments and retarding the growth of trees, flowers, and mosses. At Saihō-ji, the celebrated ground cover, a carpet of mosses more than three inches thick, has begun to change color and go bald in patches. At Katsura Palace, the serenity of Prince Tomohito's gardens is impinged upon by the steady rumble of truck traffic on a nearby highway. And at Nijo Castle, where groups of up to a thousand sightseers depart on tour at ten-minute intervals, the telltale chirping of the nightingale floors has become a perpetual cacophony.

The one structure that seems to bear heavy tourist traffic well is the oldest and most popular major temple in the city, Kiyomizu-dera. Unlike the great walled monasteries of Nishi Hongan-ji and Daitoku-ji, which sit upon the flat floor of the valley, Kiyomizu-dera perches high in the Eastern Hills, and the view from its cantilevered deck is regarded by some as the most scenic panorama in Japan. The massive timbers that

underpin the temple are said to have come from the imperial palace at Nagaoka, which would make them older than the city itself. In any event, Kammu's capital was less than a score of years old when the first structures were erected at Kiyomizu, and those buildings and their successors have stood sentinel to a millennium of history. Significantly, the great temple has been associated with each critical phase in Kyoto's history without ever becoming strongly identified with any particular epoch. As a result Kiyomizu is uniquely rich in history, treasure, and character. During the Onin War, troops were bivouacked at its base; following unification, Toyotomi Hideyoshi refurbished its art works; and during the Tokugawa ascendancy, Iemitsu underwrote a major renovation project. Shinto shrines dot its grounds, *kami* are said to invest its precincts, and mystical properties are attached to its sacred springs. Kiyomizu is the past recalled, the present given context. It is the solace and the quickpoint for countless visitors to the city that lies below it, for it belongs to all the religions of Japan and to all the ages of Kyoto.

Standing alone, at dusk, on the sloping viewing platform of Kiyomizu, the visitor to modern Kyoto often feels that time itself has been transcended. The blue flanks of Higashiyama rise on the immediate left, the soft gray domes of Arashiyama far to the right. Between them lies Kyoto, blanketed in a heavy yellow haze. This is — this can be, with only a slight limbering of the imagination — Kammu's Capital of Peace and Tranquillity. Almost twelve centuries have passed since its founding, but the allure of Kyoto's purple hills and crystal streams endures, unaltered and undiminished.

KYOTO IN LITERATURE

The splendors of the Heian era — Kyoto's true imperial epoch — have been preserved in vivid detail in the intimate, articulate, and sensitive court memoirs of an extraordinary group of eleventh-century Japanese noblewomen. Foremost among those works is the world's earliest novel, The Tale of Genji. *Lady Murasaki's discursive chronicle is matched in wit and exceeded in objectivity, however, by* The Pillow Book of Sei Shōnagon, *a contemporary commonplace book. The excerpt below, which is taken from the Ivan Morris translation of the latter work, exposes both the elegance and the decadence of Heian court life.*

The women's apartments along the gallery of the Imperial Palace are particularly pleasant. When one raises the upper part of the small half-shutters, the wind blows in extremely hard; it is cool even in summer, and in winter snow and hail come along with the wind, which I find agreeable. As the rooms are small, and as the page-boys (even though employed in such august precincts) often behave badly, we women generally stay hidden behind our screens or curtains. It is delightfully quiet there; for one cannot hear any of the loud talk and laughter that disturb one in other parts of the Palace.

Of course we must always be on the alert when we are staying in these apartments. Even during the day we cannot be off our guard, and at night we have to be especially careful. But I rather enjoy all this. Throughout the night one hears the sound of footsteps in the corridor outside. Every now and then the sound will stop, and someone will tap on a door with just a single finger. It is pleasant to think that the woman inside can instantly recognize her visitor. Sometimes the tapping will continue for quite a while without the woman's responding in any way. The man finally gives up, thinking that she must be asleep; but this does not please the woman, who makes a few cautious movements, with a rustle of silk clothes, so that her visitor will know she is really there. Then she hears him fanning himself as he remains standing outside the door.

In the winter one sometimes catches the sound of a woman gently stirring the embers in her brazier. Though she does her best to be quiet, the man who is waiting outside hears her; he knocks louder and louder, asking her to let him in. Then the woman slips furtively towards the door where she can listen to him.

On other occasions one may hear several voices reciting Chinese or Japanese poems. One of the women opens her door, though in fact no one has knocked. Seeing this, several of the men, who had no particular intention of visiting this woman, stop on their way through the gallery. Since there is no room for them all to come in, many of them spend the rest of the night out in the garden — most charming.

Bright green bamboo blinds are a delight, especially when beneath them one can make out the many layers of a woman's clothes emerging from under brilliantly coloured curtains of state. The men who glimpse this sight from the veranda, whether they be young noblemen with their over-robes informally left unsewn in the back, or Chamberlains of the Sixth Rank in their costumes of green, do not as a rule dare enter the room where the woman is seated. It is interesting to observe them as they stand there with their backs pressed to the wall and with the sleeves of their robes neatly arranged. Charming also, when one is watching from the outside, is the sight of a young man clad in laced trousers of dark purple and in a dazzling Court robe over an

The ink drawing above, like the group portrait on page 136 and the individual portraits on pages 140–59, comes from The Thirty-six Immortal Poets *screen.*

array of varicoloured garments, as he leans forward into the woman's room, pushing aside the green blind. . . .

I particularly enjoy the rehearsal before the Special Festival when I am staying in the women's apartments at the Palace. As the men from the Office of Grounds walk along, they hold their long pine torches high above them; because of the cold their heads are drawn into their robes, and consequently the ends of the torches are always threatening to bump into things. Soon there is the pleasant sound of music as the players pass outside the women's apartments playing their flutes. Some of the young noblemen in the Palace, fascinated by the scene, appear in their Court costumes and stand outside our rooms chatting with us, while their attendants quietly order people to make way for their masters. All the voices mingle with the music in an unfamiliar and delightful way.

Since the night is already well advanced, one does not bother to go to bed but waits for the dawn when the musicians and dancers return from their rehearsal. . . .

Almost everyone enjoys these things; but occasionally some sober-sides will hurry by, without stopping to watch the scene. Then one of the women calls out laughingly to him, 'Wait a moment, Sir! How can you abandon the charms of such a night? Stay for a while and enjoy yourself!' But evidently the man is in a bad mood, for he scurries along the corridor, almost tumbling over himself in his haste, as though in terror of being pursued and captured.

SEI SHONAGON
The Pillow Book of Sei Shōnagon, c. 1002

Engelbertus Kaempfer, a physician attached to the Dutch embassy that reached Japan during the closing decades of the seventeenth century, also acted as that expedition's unofficial chronicler. The bulk of Kaempfer's History of Japan *is naturally devoted to Edo, which had been the effective seat of political power in Japan since 1603. However, his annals do include an account of his party's journey to Kyoto, western terminus of the fabled Tōkaidō Road. During the Tokugawa period, Japan's hereditary nobility lived within the royal enclosure at "Kio," which Kaempfer describes in unadorned prose.*

Kio, or *Miaco* . . . signifies in Japanese a city. It is so call'd by way of pre-eminence, being the residence of his holiness the *Dairi*, or Ecclesiastical hereditary Emperor, and on this account reckon'd the capital of the whole Empire. It lies in the Province *Jamatto* [Yamato], in a large plain, and is from North to South three quarters of a German mile long, and half a German mile broad from East to West. It is surrounded with pleasant green hills and mountains, on which arise numbers of small rivers and agreeable springs. The city comes nearest the mountains on the East-side, where there are abundance of temples, monasteries, chapels, and other religious buildings, standing in the ascent, which we shall have an opportunity to survey to and describe more accurately upon our return. Three shallow rivers enter, or run by the city on that side; the chief and largest comes out of the Lake of *Oitz*; the two others fall down from the neighbouring mountains, and they are all united into one, about the middle of the city, where there is a large bridge, two hundred paces long, call'd *Sensjonosas*, laid over it. From thence the united stream takes its course Westward. The *Dairi*, with his Ecclesiastical family and court, resides on the North-side of the city, in a particular part or ward, consisting of twelve or thirteen streets, and separate from the city by walls and ditches. In the Western part of the town, is a strong castle built of free stone. It was built by one of the Ecclesiastical hereditary Emperors, for the security of his person, during the civil wars; and at present it serves to lodge the secular monarch, when he comes to visit the *Dairi*. It is an hundred and fifty *Kins* or fathoms long, where longest. A deep ditch fill'd with water, and wall'd in, surrounds it, and is enclos'd it self by a broad empty space, or dry ditch. In the middle of this castle, there is as usual, a square, tower several stories high. In the ditch are kept a particular sort of delicious carps, some of which were presented this evening to our Interpreter. A small garrison guards the castle, under the command of a captain. The streets are narrow, but all regular, running some South, some East. Being at one end of a great street, it is impossible to reach the other with the eye, because of their extraordinary length, the dust, and the multitude of people they are daily crowded with. The houses are, generally speaking, narrow, only two stories high, built of wood, lime and clay, according to the country fashion, and the roofs cover'd with shavings of wood. A wooden trough fill'd with water, with the necessary instruments for extinguishing fires, lie ready at all times at the tops of the houses. *Miaco* is the great magazine of all Japanese manufactures and commodities, and the chief mercantile town in the Empire. There is scarce a house in this large capital, where there is not something made or sold. Here they refine copper, coin money, print books, weave the richest stuffs with gold and silver flowers. The best and scarcest dies, the most artful carvings, all sorts of musical Instruments, pictures, japan'd cabinets, all sorts of things wrought in gold and other metals, particularly in steel, as the best temper'd blades, and other arms are made here in the utmost perfection, as are also the richest dresses, and after the best fashion, all sorts of toys, puppets, moving their heads of themselves, and numberless other things, too many to be here mention'd. In short, there is nothing can be thought of, but what may be found at *Miaco*, and nothing, tho' never so neatly wrought, can be imported from abroad, but what some artist or other in this capital will undertake to imitate. Considering this, it is no wonder that the manufactures of *Miaco* are become so famous throughout the Empire, as to be easily preferr'd to all others, tho' perhaps inferior in some particulars, only because they have the name of being made at *Kio*. There are but few houses in all the chief streets, where there is not something to be sold, and for my part, I could not help admiring, whence they can have customers enough for such an immense quantity of goods. 'Tis true indeed, there is scarce any body passes through *Miaco*, but what buys something or other of the manufactures of this city, either for his own use or for presents to be made to his friends and relations. The Lord chief Justice [Shogun] resides at *Miaco*, a man of great power and authority, as having the supreme command, under the Emperor, of all the *Bugjo's*, Governors, Stewards and other Officers, who are any ways concern'd in the government of the Imperial cities, crown lands and tenements, in all the Western Provinces of the Empire. Even the Western Princes themselves must in some measure depend of him.

ENGELBERTUS KAEMPFER
History of Japan, 1693

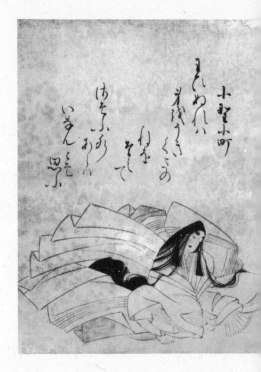

While studying law in London in the 1880's, the Japanese author of the following excerpt was virtually adopted by a kind professor and his wife. After completing his studies and returning to his homeland, D. C. Angus — as he now styled himself — set down his childhood reminiscences in the form of an extended letter to his English hosts' youngest child, Nelly. As an impressionable youth, Angus recalls, he joined his uncle on a visit to the old imperial capital of "Kioto" — a heady experience cut short by the arrival of distressing news from home.

When I reached Kioto, the people and place seemed to me enchanted; and I thought of the Shogun as the sorcerer who kept them spell-bound. Without the palace gates were war and tumult, within was intrigue; but peace and pleasure seemed to lull the courtiers and their master into a slumberous state, in which "it was always afternoon." But I was too young and obscure to know of the forces at work around and within, which were even then breaking the magic sleep.

For the next few months my life, as I look back on it, seems to have been one long spring within and without. It was spring in my heart; and favouring circumstances made it blossom into joy, just as young plants grow strong and beautiful in the soft showers and warm sunlight of May. You must excuse these poetic bursts of mine, Nelly. I remember that you and your brothers used to call them "soft." That they may be; but it is as natural to a Japanese boy to feel and express these things, as to an English boy, if he feels them, to repress them.

My kind protector presented me to one of the learned Shinto priest nobles, as worthy of encouragement, and I became his reverent pupil.

I practised knightly games with the youths, and played chequers or chess with the young ladies of the court; and we all, young and old, delighted in games of wit and poetry, improvisations and story-telling, for which there were prizes and hard-fought contests. At night there were stately court dances, and we often got up "pageants," at which we wore suitable masks and costumes for the characters represented. I, as one of the poets of the court, and as "great on history," had much to do with the planning of these, and I was assisted by the quick wit of one of the young ladies, who was as often victor as vanquished in our improvising and punning games. In the longer poetic contests I also often came off winner, since from my great love of our ancient legends I could make a hit at a subject while the others were casting about for theirs, and I had for some time been studying composition and verse-making. Story-telling, too, brought me into favour with many who first looked down on the boy my master had picked up — "no family, quite a wonder he has any manners at all."

I wrote, in fact, one or two tales and patriotic ballads, which were thought worthy of being laid at the Mikado's [Emperor's] feet; and as he deigned to approve them, and to send me in token of his condescension a gold-mounted fan and jewelled sword-scabbard, I came into high favour at the court for a little while.

Kioto is a beautiful city, lying high amid green hills and mountains, near to lake Biwa, and surrounded by fair gardens, and clear rivers whose branches flow down some of the city streets. It is not so gloomily imposing as castellated Yedo [Tokyo], but is a bright, cheerful, sunny place of groves, temples, and palaces, squares and monasteries. The Mikado's palace (like his dress and surroundings) was distinguished by refined simplicity rather than pomp and magnificence. And Kioto prided itself on taking the court tone in this and other particulars. As for the Mikado, it was thought that display was unbefitting one so great as to be far above the need of imposing on the world by it; while his courtiers . . . were content to despise . . . the daimios. . . .

The society of Kioto took after the court pattern, and was simple, refined, and charming. The ladies had an air and style which no one out of Kioto could equal. Learned men flocked to the capital, where there was leisure to enjoy their gifts; and all that was most chivalrous, gentle, and accomplished in manners and arts, was drawn to Kioto and found within it.

But, Nelly, do you think that when in Kioto, and a favourite at court, I ever once *saw* the Emperor whom I revered so much? No such thing. For hundreds of years the Mikado had never been seen by anyone but his wives and chief ministers. The *people* never even saw the screen or curtain that hid him from the general court. If he went outside the palace gates, it was in a closely curtained litter drawn by bullocks; but that was rare. He lived his life in the palace and its gardens, or in the summer palace in the park behind, walled from human eyes, where an intruder would have met instant death. His feet never touched the ground. Piled up mats made the imperial throne, and wherever he placed his feet contact with common earth or flooring was prevented by the anxious attendants. His name was so sacred that people of our station never pronounced it aloud or wrote it in full.

This was the unseen being to whom our loyalty clung.

It had not always been so; but at this time the Mikados had been for centuries the slaves and victims of their greatness — shut out by Eastern habits and the harem-life from healthy activity and contact with the world, till they lost the power to will, and were often little better than puppets in the hands of their female relations, their ministers, or courtiers.

A strange and sudden end came to my gay spring-time in Kioto; to the picnics to the blue lake Biwa, where we stayed in rustic summer houses and composed rhapsodies on the scenery; to the "chamber of inspiring view" in my chief's house (my favourite resort as a poet); to the tournament by day, and dances by night; to the songs and jests and laughter.

A flying post brought me one day a letter from Hana. To my dismay, it contained only a few hurried lines, entreating me to return instantly, as great trouble had befallen them. My uncle, having gone out one evening, and being expected home in about an hour, had then been three days absent, sending no letter or sign, and all search and enquiry had hitherto been fruitless. Of course I returned as quickly as possible, and found trouble worse than I had dreamt of awaiting me. With closed doors and in low whispers I was told that there was little hope that my uncle's disappearance could be accidental — that spies had been seen about the house for weeks, and that my mother and the neighbours thought it was certain that he had been seized in some lonely place when off his guard, and secretly imprisoned, or worse, by Government.

"Surely, when off his guard," I answered, "or he would not have failed to perform hara-kiri rather than be taken living. But why imprisoned? what could *he* have done, who was so wise and just?"

The answer came falteringly, Hana turning paler: "We believe he has turned Christian."

D. C. ANGUS
Japan, the Eastern Wonderland, 1910

KYOTO'S FUGITIVE CHARMS

Born in Greece of British parents and raised in the United States, nineteenth-century author and essayist Lafcadio Hearn came to Japan by the most circuitous of geographical and cultural routes. Once there, however, he put down firm roots, taking both a Japanese wife and a Japanese name, Koizumi Yakumo. The writer's lyrical evocations of life under the Meiji Emperor played a vital role in introducing Japanese culture to the West. It is somehow altogether proper that Hearn, who celebrated "the fugitive charm of Japanese amusements," should find himself in Kyoto in 1894 — the festival year marking the eleven-hundredth anniversary of the city's founding.

It had been intended to celebrate in spring the eleven hundredth anniversary of the foundation of Kyōto; but the outbreak of pestilence caused postponement of the festival to the autumn, and the celebration began on the 15th of the tenth month. Little festival medals of nickel, made to be pinned to the breast, like military decorations, were for sale at half a yen each. These medals entitled the wearers to special cheap fares on all the Japanese railroad and steamship lines, and to other desirable privileges, such as free entrance to wonderful palaces, gardens, and temples. On the 23d of October I found myself in possession of a medal, and journeying to Kyōto by the first morning train, which was overcrowded with people eager to witness the great historical processions announced for the 24th and 25th. Many had to travel standing, but the crowd was good-natured and merry. A number of my fellow-passengers were Ōsaka geisha going to the festival. They diverted themselves by singing songs and by playing ken with some male acquaintances, and their kittenish pranks and funny cries kept everybody amused. One had an extraordinary voice, with which she could twitter like a sparrow....

The first surprise with which Kyōto greeted her visitors was the beauty of her festival decorations. Every street had been prepared for illumination. Before each house had been planted a new lantern-post of unpainted wood, from which a lantern bearing some appropriate design was suspended. There were also national flags and sprigs of pine above each entrance. But the lanterns made the charm of the display. In each section of street they were of the same form, and were fixed at exactly the same height, and were protected from possible bad weather by the same kind of covering. But in different streets the lanterns were different. In some of the wide thoroughfares they were very large; and while in some streets each was sheltered by a little wooden awning, in others every lantern had a Japanese paper umbrella spread and fastened above it.

There was no pageant on the morning of my arrival, and I spent a couple of hours delightfully at the festival exhibition of kakemono [hanging scrolls] in the imperial summer palace called Omuro Gosho. Unlike the professional art display which I had seen in the spring, this represented chiefly the work of students; and I found it incomparably more original and attractive. Nearly all the pictures, thousands in number, were for sale, at prices ranging from three to fifty yen; and it was impossible not to buy to the limit of one's purse. There were studies of nature evidently made on the spot: such as a glimpse of hazy autumn ricefields, with dragonflies darting over the drooping grain; maples crimsoning above a tremendous gorge; ranges of peaks steeped in morning mist; and a peasant's cottage perched on the verge of some dizzy mountain road. Also there were fine bits of realism, such as a cat seizing a mouse in the act of stealing the offerings placed in a Buddhist household shrine.

But I have no intention to try the reader's patience with a description of pictures. I mention my visit to the display only because of something I saw there more interesting than any picture. Near the main entrance was a specimen of handwriting, intended to be mounted as a kakemono later on, and temporarily fixed upon a board about three feet long by eighteen inches wide, — a Japanese poem. It was a wonder of calligraphy. Instead of the usual red stamp or seal with which the Japanese calligrapher marks his masterpieces, I saw the red imprint of a tiny, tiny hand, — a *living* hand, which had been smeared with crimson printing-ink and deftly pressed upon the paper. I could distinguish those little finger-marks of which Mr. Galton has taught us the characteristic importance.

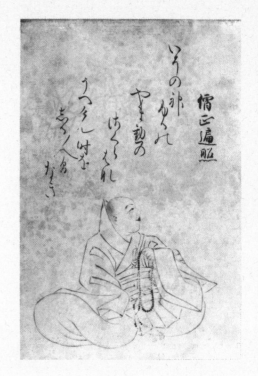

That writing had been done in the presence of His Imperial Majesty by a child of six years, — or of five, according to our Western method of computing age from the date of birth. The prime minister, Marquis Ito, saw the miracle, and adopted the little boy, whose present name is therefore Ito Medzui.

Even Japanese observers could scarcely believe the testimony of their own eyes. Few adult calligraphers could surpass that writing. Certainly no Occidental artist, even after years of study, could repeat the feat performed by the brush of that child before the Emperor. Of course such a child can be born but once in a thousand years, — to realize, or almost realize, the ancient Chinese legends of divinely inspired writers.

Still, it was not the beauty of the thing in itself which impressed me, but the weird, extraordinary indubitable proof it afforded of an inherited memory so vivid as to be almost equal to the recollection of former births. Generations of dead calligraphers revived in the fingers of that tiny hand. The thing was never the work of an individual child five years old, but beyond all question the work of ghosts, — the countless ghosts that make the compound ancestral soul. It was proof visible and tangible of psychological and physiological wonders justifying both the Shinto doctrine of ancestor worship and the Buddhist doctrine of preëxistence.

After looking at all the pictures I visited the great palace garden, only recently opened to the public. It is called the Garden of the Cavern of the Genii. (At least "genii" is about the only word one can use to translate the term "Sennin," for which there is no real English equivalent; the Sennin, who are supposed to possess immortal life, and to haunt forests or caverns, being Japanese, or rather Chinese mythological transformations of the Indian Rishi.) The garden deserves its name. I felt as if I had indeed entered an enchanted place.

It is a landscape-garden, — a Buddhist creation, belonging to what is now simply a palace, but was once a monastery, built as a religious retreat for emperors and princes weary of earthly vanities. (The first impression received after passing the gate is that of a grand old English park: the colossal trees, the shorn grass, the broad walks, the fresh sweet scent of verdure, all awaken English memories. . . .)

Considered as a human work alone, the garden is a marvel: only the skilled labor of thousands could have joined together the mere bones of it, the prodigious rocky skeleton of its plan. This once shaped and earthed and planted, Nature was left alone to finish the wonder. Working through ten centuries, she has surpassed — nay, unspeakably magnified — the dream of the artist. Without exact information, no stranger unfamiliar with the laws and the purpose of Japanese garden-construction could imagine that all this had a human designer some thousand years ago: the effect is that of a section of primeval forest, preserved untouched from the beginning, and walled away from the rest of the world in the heart of the old capital. The rock-faces, the great fantastic roots, the shadowed by-paths, the few ancient graven monoliths, are all cushioned with the moss of ages; and climbing things have developed stems a foot thick, that hang across spaces like monstrous serpents. Parts of the garden vividly recall some aspects of tropical nature in the Antilles; — though one misses the palms, the bewildering web and woof of lianas, the reptiles, and the sinister day-silence of a West Indian forest. The joyous storm of bird life overhead is an astonishment, and proclaims gratefully to the visitor that the wild creatures of this monastic paradise have never been harmed or frightened by man. As I arrived at last, with regret, at the gate of exit, I could not help feeling envious of its keeper: only to be a servant in such a garden were a privilege well worth praying for. . . .

I passed the evening wandering through the illuminated streets, and visited some of the numberless shows. I saw a young man writing Buddhist texts and drawing horses with his feet; the extraordinary fact about the work being that the texts were written backwards, — from the bottom of the column up, just as an ordinary calligrapher would write them from the top of the column down, — and the pictures of horses were always commenced with the tail. I saw a kind of amphitheatre, with an aquarium in lieu of arena, where mermaids swam and sang Japanese songs. I saw maidens "made by glamour out of flowers" by a Japanese cultivator of chrysanthemums. And between whiles I peeped into the toy-shops, full of novelties. What there especially struck me was the display of that astounding ingenuity by which Japanese inventors are able to reach, at a cost too small to name, precisely the same results as those exhibited in our expensive mechanical toys. A group of cocks and hens made of paper were set to pecking imaginary grain out of a basket by the pressure of a bamboo spring, — the whole thing costing half a cent. An artificial mouse ran about, doubling and scurrying, as if trying to slip under mats or into chinks: it cost only one cent, and was made with a bit of colored paper, a spool of baked clay and a long thread; you had only to pull the thread, and the mouse began to run. Butterflies of paper, moved by an equally simple device, began to fly when thrown into the air. An artificial cuttlefish began to wriggle all its tentacles when you blew into a little rush tube fixed under its head.

When I decided to return, the lanterns were out, the shops were closing; and the streets darkened about me long before I reached the hotel. After the great glow of the illumination, the witchcrafts of the shows, the merry tumult, the sea-like sound of wooden sandals, this sudden coming of blankness and silence made me feel as if the previous experience had been unreal, — an illusion of light and color and noise made just to deceive, as in stories of goblin foxes. But the quick vanishing of all that composes a Japanese festival-night really lends a keener edge to the pleasure of remembrance: there is no slow fading out of the phantasmagoria, and its memory is thus kept free from the least tinge of melancholy.

LAFCADIO HEARN
Gleanings in Buddha-Fields, 1897

*Baron Albert d'Anethan, scion of an ancient and distinguished Belgian family,
assumed his ambassadorial post in Tokyo on the eve of the Sino-Japanese War
of 1894 — and departed fourteen years later, having weathered a succession of
diplomatic storms. Those tension-fraught years were the subject of a personal
diary maintained by Baroness d'Anethan, a formidable woman who brought a
keen eye and a certain moral rectitude to her task.*

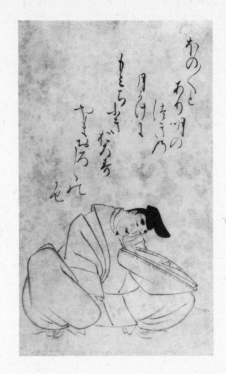

I am perfectly enchanted with Kyoto. So far I have seen no place in Japan
that can compare with this beautiful city, either in the antiquity and interest
of its temples and their romantic surroundings, or in its more natural beauties of wooded hills and of luxuriant vegetation. Kyoto was for many years
the seat of the almost-forgotten Emperors. As one realises the charm of this
unique city, it certainly seems a thousand pities that the event of the Restoration should have been the means of transferring the capital to Tokyo, a city
which — in spite of its many advantages — possesses, with exception of its
moated ramparts of stone and its uncommon and handsome gateways, but
few architectural objects of interest, being placed in flat, fen-like surroundings of paddy-fields, by no means either beautiful or healthy. Now, Kyoto
is really "Old Japan," and, thank goodness! there are no smells! Yaami's
Hotel, where we are staying, is beautifully situated. It is a great climb to get
to it, but once there, one has before one's eyes a perfect view of the city
and the distant hills.

April 22, 1895. — We went, accompanied by two friends, to see the procession of the unfortunate girls of the Yoshiwara [red-light district]. This procession takes place once a year, and to witness it there were enormous crowds,
most interesting to watch, packed in masses and squatting down on their
mats. We had to wait for over two hours and a half before the girls arrived.
At last they came — fourteen of them — one by one, walking their slow
walk, raised on their high *geta* (pattens), and dressed in gorgeous embroi-
deries, while the *obi*, the huge stiff bows of which were tied in front, a sign
of their unfortunate profession, was of the richest brocade. The head-dress
worn was truly wonderful, rather like a Norwegian head-dress, with the
exception that huge pins of different descriptions, jade, coral, lacquer, etc.,
were stuck in the hair in all directions, like formidable weapons of defence.
The faces of the girls were daubed with white paint, and they wore a fixed,
set expression, while their eyes never moved. Each courtesan was preceded by
two children, likewise adorned in magnificent *kimonos*, the courtesans themselves each being escorted by an old woman, who is supposed to act the part
of a mother, and who every now and then with deft fingers arranged the
hair or beautiful dress. . . . It was a painful sight, though one could see, by the
immense crowds gathered to witness it, this yearly procession is here looked
upon as an interesting spectacle.

On leaving this quarter of the town we were accompanied by ten policemen to clear the way, the crowd being hustled and shouted at, till I begged
for mercy for the poor inoffensive beings.

April 23, 1895. — Mr. Tuke came and took us sightseeing. Among other
places we drove to the Kyo-Midzu Temple, which is built on immense
wooden piles, and from which we had glorious views of Kyoto and its distant
hills, while far beneath, from the deep ravine, rose a wealth of varied and
fragrant vegetation.

We went in the evening, with one of the officials of the Imperial Household, to see the far-famed cherry dance. It was certainly a lovely sight. About forty girls, gorgeously adorned, went through their peculiar but graceful motions, framed by beautiful and ever-changing scenery. The *geishas* arrive on the stage from both sides of the theatre, enacting picturesque scenes, which are supposed to represent each of the seasons. On this occasion they finished up with summer, the scene being laid in a romantic and fairy-like Japanese garden, lit up with lanterns and thousands of different coloured lamps. The stage arrangement and *mise en scène* generally were quite lovely. . . .

April 26, 1895. — We went to see the Nijo Palace, built by Iyeyasu in 1601. It is necessary to have special permission to inspect this palace. It is, as Murray calls it, "a dream of golden beauty." A magnificent gate, very seldom used, and the entrance by which was a special privilege, was opened for us; it was gorgeous with gold and curious carvings. After having signed our names in the book, we were shown all over the spacious rooms and audience halls. The decorations on the walls are particularly magnificent, bold and grand on a gold ground, the wood being cryptomeria and hinoki. The ceilings are very handsome and of precious woods. The most impressive apartment is the hall of audience. It simply blazes with gold, and the metal fastenings are gilt and of exquisite workmanship, while the painting of the pine trees on the walls is extremely striking. In every room the painting on the walls is varied — cherry blossom, birds, tigers, chrysanthemums, lilies, etc. — all beautifully and artistically depicted on a blazing gold ground.

In the afternoon we witnessed a so-called religious procession, one of the most curious spectacles imaginable. We were deposited by our guide in a tea-house to watch the procession pass. Half a dozen gorgeously painted cars or shrines attached to long poles were carried by scores of semi-naked men, shouting and yelling, screaming and scrambling. These men, who advanced at a jog-trot, were employed in jerking the shrine up and down with violent, spasmodic jumps. There was an interval of about five minutes between the arrival of each of these huge shrines, and as each appeared round the corner the same mad scene repeated itself. There were a few priests on horseback accompanying the shrines, but the chief objects of interest were the brilliantly decorated shrines themselves, within the shelter of which was supposed to be reposing some unfortunate god, who surely must have suffered from a severe attack of sea-sickness as a result of the energy displayed.

April 27, 1895. — E. and I drove to the Kinkakuji Gardens, within which is placed a monastery, and a pavilion which is supposed to be golden. So far as I could see, there was but very little gold left. The garden itself is, however, a perfect dream of beauty. It is wonderfully laid out, with bridges and streams and winding paths, and in the midst is a lake studded with lovely little islands, while golden carp and venerable tortoises, perfectly tame, disport themselves in the water. . . .

May 3, 1895. — We left Kyoto in a reserved carriage, accompanied by three policemen. This protection was provided for us by the Government, who feared possible unpleasantness for foreigners owing to the intervention of Russia, France, and Germany with regard to the territory claimed by Japan from China, which claim, in spite of her victorious war, she was consequently reluctantly forced by the Powers to abandon.

BARONESS ALBERT D'ANETHAN
Fourteen Years of Diplomatic Life in Japan, 1912

"Neither am I nourished by fleshless, abstract memories," Nikos Kazantzakis *declares — and his highly personalized vision of Kyoto is anything but a reiteration of stale history and familiar statistics. The Greek novelist gathered his observations in the course of a midnight ramble through the entertainment quarter of Japan's "capital of peace." "Every city has its sex," he assures the reader, and this one is "all female." Coming from Kazantzakis, that is perhaps the ultimate compliment.*

I will never forget the long, narrow streets of Kyoto in nighttime with their innumerable multicolored lanterns; the scented air whistled, laughed, and sometimes a gong from a Buddhist temple sounded sweetly, discreetly, and behind the green reed walls were heard the hard, nervous chords of a samisen with the sad song of a woman:

> *And at the night that the snow falls*
> *And at the night that all drink tea*
> *If you love me, come, I beg you....*

Or another eternal Saphian craving of a woman:

> *All this long, long night,*
> *Long as the tail of a golden pheasant,*
> *Well, it is written for me to sleep alone.*

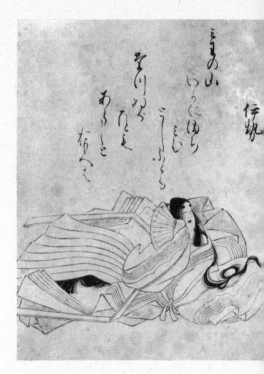

I had gone astray, without knowing it, in the alleys where the geishas live and saw smiling old women — old veterans who work now as doorwomen and welcome the men and help them take off their sandals and open for them the small inside door.... I stayed for a while at an open door. I bent down and looked in at the tiny yard. Blooming flowers in the pots, a fragrance of aromatic wood, two big paper lanterns underneath three broad wooden steps.... And on them shoes of all sorts placed in order. And another row of sandals and slippers hastily placed in a disorderly fashion. Certainly on this long night, long as the tail of a golden pheasant, the geishas — thank God — will not sleep alone.

I saunter until long after midnight, I feel too sorry to close my eyes. It seems to me that all this spring mirage is a nocturnal performance of a city in which Maras, the god of human delusion, is raised in the air for a moment. He will now blow, and everything — lanterns, temples, men, wooden sandals — will vanish. I go back and forth in order to see the architecture of the mirage while it is still there. This, then, is Heian-kyo, the "capital of peace," where the emperors of Nara took refuge in 794 in order to be saved from the powerful and greedy priests! In vain! The same refined and lascivious priests were the courtiers of the new palace in Kyoto. The same flowers of evil: Chinese fashions, shameless waste, piety and debauchery. The memorandum an honest courtier submitted to Emperor Daigo still exists: "The monks are inhuman, they do not care about religion, they have mistresses, they make counterfeit money, they steal and rob, they eat meat and violate all the orders." The noblemen spent their time composing verses, riddles, puzzles, arranging flowers, organizing holidays for the celebration of the cherry-blossom trees, the full moon, the water.... They covered the trees with flowers during the winter and with snow in the summer. They were crazy about dogs and cats, which were given official titles and many servants. When the king's favorite cat gave birth, the courtiers sent presents to it — silk ribbons or small mice on a golden tray.

As I pass through the streets of this city, at night, I look at them as I would at a beloved person in the darkness. Every city has its sex, male or female. This one is all female. I recount its love adventures, its scandals, its lavishness and luxuries — and everything seems to me sacred and necessary. This city has performed its duty as a woman. It helped the people to make progress with its fatal feminine method: loving, wasting, raising luxury, perhaps, to its true height — the holy position of necessity.

I am glad that I have found, wandering the streets, the essence and the mission of this old, sinful city. This city gave for the final creation of the Japanese soul its feminine cell. I am glad that tomorrow morning when we both awaken and she will be uncovered before me in the sunlight, I will know why I should love her, forgiving all her sins, as a sinful woman who loves too much should also be forgiven.

May this lavishness, what we call luxury, excess, extravagance, be blessed! Civilization means to feel luxury as necessity, to surpass the animal by not being satisfied only with food, drink, sleep and woman. At the moment that the "wingless biped" craves for the unnecessary luxury, as he would for bread, he begins to become man. Whatever good this world has, whatever has been saved from the human masses, is luxury: a painting, a carved flower, a song, an idea beyond the average mind. Luxury is the greatest necessity of the superior man. The excess of his heart. That is the true heart.

I saunter the endless sumptuous palaces of this city that has been the capital for a thousand years. I stop at the "Blue and Cool Room," the steps of which have been so artfully placed that when the distant breeze of the Lake Biwa blows, the room is cooled. I enjoy the paintings — birds, flowers, waters, reeds; the statues; the inscriptions; and the royal drapes with the three sacred colors, red, white and black. On the walls there are wise sayings of Confucius: *The king is like the wind; the people are like the grass. The grass must bend when the wind passes.* The wind passed, the grass withered away — only the saying remained.

I passed through the deserted royal palaces that even the spiders do not inhabit. The kings died and only the sacred royal emblem, the chrysanthemum with sixteen petals, remains carved on ivory, on gold, on wood, or painted on the folding screens and fans. I pass through the gardens; I think that there is no more beautiful sight in the world than a Chinese or a Japanese garden, one of the highest peaks of wisdom and sensitivity that man has reached. . . .

I wander around the museums, I look at the Japanese paintings, I insatiably admire the simplicity and the power, the inexpressible frugality of each line. That is the true art — bare, without vain adornments and gaudy colors. I look graspingly and warn myself: never forget these reeds that Kano Tanyu painted; remember well the refinement, the few gray-silver colors, the black, slight firm line — and the reed that bends immortally over the invisible water. . . .

Never forget this fire of Buntso Tani. We hear fire, we see flames, we burn. But we don't understand. Suddenly we see this very fire and immediately we feel deeply the essence of fire. We are terrified.

Farther on, in a portrait on the wall, a hermit in orange garments sits and gazes at Nothing. Still further, five monks dressed in red, sitting in a row at the terrace of the monastery, quietly and decisively look at the empty air, smiling. A wooden Kannon, the goddess of mercy, rises in a corner with a multitude of hands. And every hand has a different expression: it pushes, it holds, it caresses, it points out, it chases, it begs. . . . But her main hands are tightly joined into prayer. . . . Gardens, secrets of script, tea parties, arrangements of flowers — tender springs of joy that cannot rise from the bosom of white man. The yellow race is much more delicate than ours, and simultaneously, in a mysterious combination, more barbarous. Their traditions and history are sometimes full of fantastic sensitivity and of brutal cruelty.

In the Buddhist temple where I wandered today in Hono-zi, Nobunaga, one of the greatest warriors, statesmen and revelers ever born in Japan, was killed in 1582. A gigantic soul, highest in wisdom, first in drink and in war, and first in pleasure. He feared neither gods nor men. Tough, silent, he wanted to destroy theocracy, bring back peace and order to his country, save men from the gods. He dashed with his army to the richest and most sacred Buddhist monastery, Lieizan, opposite Kyoto. It was a beautiful city, a powerful religious center. "Go forth! Burn it!" shouted Nobunaga. The soldiers trembled and did not dare. "Burn it, the earth must be cleansed," again shouted the fearful leader. The monastery was reduced to ashes, thousands of monks and women and children were slain.

But one night when Nobunaga was feasting, he grabbed the head of his friend, Mitsushide, and derisively drummed his iron fan on his friend's forehead. Mitsushide accepted the insult smiling; but one night he took his friends and made for the temple of Hono-zi, where Nobunaga lived. The terrible tyrant appeared at the window and a torrent of arrows pierced him. He crawled inside, and as he felt the end of his life had come, he slew his wife and children and committed hara-kiri. He used to say, "Man dies once. Life is brief and the world is a dream; Let's die gloriously!"

The voices that sang were lost together with the throats, the harp- and flute-playing fingers rotted away along with the dancing feet. And only the paintings and statues, which fill the human heart with happiness, still remain in all these monasteries: a religious ecstasy, an immovable paradisian air, hermits with heads erect against the moonlight, spirits that pass over the earth like frost. And simultaneously, the most keen observations of life, a warm representation of the smallest detail, humor, joy, love of everyday life, colors — a golden rooster in a white landscape covered with snow. . . .

There is a deep mystery in these paintings — suggestive, penetrating, a light dream-atmosphere. They are never copies of nature, regardless of how faithful they look; they always project the object they represent. You feel that the painter loves the external form, but loves still more the mystic forces that gave birth to the form. He paints the invisible through the only means he has in his command: by faithfully representing the visible. "Render the spiritual life through the rhythm of things!" ordered an old Chinese saint.

The white man finds his supreme joy by pitting himself against the surrounding world as well as by imposing his ego and subjugating the natural forces to his task. The Oriental finds his supreme joy by plunging into his world and harmonizing his individual rhythm with that of the world. Today I enjoy this deep inner contrast between the two races while looking at the Japanese paintings. The main or central theme of Japanese painting is never the man whom we see painted; it is the air around him, the landscape, the mystic contact of his soul with the tree, the water, the cloud. The main theme is: brotherhood, identification, or, better, the return of man to his own world.

NIKOS KAZANTZAKIS
Japan, China, 1963

In 1931, the year that Mao Tse-tung established a Communist government in Kiangsi province, Chiang Yee was a district governor in his native China. Two years later he emigrated to England, where he soon launched a second career, this one as author and illustrator of a series of volumes on Chinese poetry and painting. Over the years Chiang also published a dozen travelogues, none more fascinating than The Silent Traveller in Japan, *in which the prolific writer draws upon his firsthand knowledge of China's ancient capitals to amplify his description of Kyoto.*

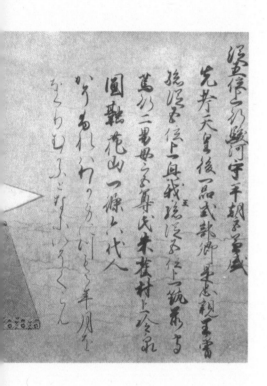

The Gion area is a special quarter of Kyoto having its own type of two-story houses with wooden-lace fronts lining both sides of the rather narrow streets. The layout of Kyoto city was said to be based on that of Ch'ang-an, the famous Chinese capital of the T'ang period. I have never been to Ch'ang-an in Shen-si Province and cannot say whether the old residence quarter outside the ancient palace is in fact similar to the Gion center, but I remember that some houses with two low stories in Soochow, Hangchow, and in the southern part of old Nanking are somewhat similar, though the Chinese houses are usually built of bricks, not wood. Many two-story houses on one side of Kamo River with the geisha or maiko girls leaning on the wooden railing on the upper story reminded me very much of those houses along the river Ch'in-huai on the southern part of old Nanking. Nanking was a famous capital during the whole epoch of the Six Dynasties (220–589) and that part of the river Ch'in-huai was lined with the houses of courtesans. The many beautiful and gifted courtesans attracted wealthy folk and men of letters to spend a gay life of entertainment with music, songs, and wine as much or even more, one imagines, than the geisha girls at Gion during the Heian period, although those geisha and maiko girls were not exactly courtesans.

Many beautiful stories and poems have been written about the river Ch'in-huai, on which flowery boats carrying poets, singsong girls, and banquet tables moved slowly up and down the river. The gaiety of life of those early days in Nanking has been handed down to the present, though conditions are far different from what they used to be. When I was a college student in Nanking, a few friends and I once hired a boat with wine, food, and musicians to glide on the river, but the dirty look of both shores, the smelly water, and the dilapidated railings and walls of the houses from which beautiful girls could easily fall at any moment rather disgusted me. I went there in order to see how the gay life, as described in Chinese stories and poems, might have been conducted in those early years, but I got no illusion at all. Here in Gion of Kyoto, though it may have been modified somewhat, I can imagine the way of life that has been led since the Heian days. Here, as I said at the beginning, everyone seems to be intent on contributing his or her effort to keep the past of Kyoto alive. This is a well-organized business that has kept modern Kyoto still the old Kyoto. . . .

Among all the places I have seen in Kyoto, my experience up on Kiyomizudera-ji still lingers in my mind vividly. . . . The Kiyomizudera Temple is built on a promontory at the western foot of Higashiyama Hill, on higher ground unlike the other temples on the plains. The first structure was made at the beginning of the ninth century but the present one, dating back to 1633, is a replica of its main hall. Though the temple itself was on higher ground, the main hall was higher still, built on many stilt poles of solid wood joined together to support the wide wooden platform, with wooden railings all round. From there I enjoyed a far more extensive panoramic view of the city than from the metal tower near Kyoto station. The beauty of this view is the sight of the temple standing above all the different kinds of trees in many shades of fresh green, with cherry blossoms here and there appearing among them. There are well-paved stone steps, and a number of Japanese women in colored kimonos dotting the scene everywhere; the whole view is the sight of the temple standing above all the different kinds of trees me as I walked about, and I made a few rough sketches here and there in order to illustrate the views I failed to describe in words.

CHIANG YEE
The Silent Traveller in Japan, 1972

THE FLORENCE OF JAPAN

It was anthropology that brought the Florentine scholar Fosco Maraini to Japan in 1938 — to study the Ainu, the aboriginal people of the northern islands. But it was politics that kept him there, for following the collapse of Italy in 1943 Maraini and other Italian nationals were interned not far from Kyoto. Returning to Kyoto many years later, Maraini was to note both the aesthetic and geophysical similarities between the old capital and his native Florence.

This morning I climbed up into the wood behind the Silvery Water. . . . Kyoto lay below, in the uncertain sunlight of a morning ready at any moment to dissolve into rain. The flat expanse of roofs lay like a grey fjord between the mountains, broken here and there by the mass of a Buddhist temple or the elegant tower of a pagoda. Kyoto is the only major Japanese city which was not practically wiped out in the 1945 air-raids. The Japanese had the good sense not to have military objectives there, and the Americans, thanks above all to the representations of the noted orientalist Serge Elisséev, spared it. From where I was sitting the view of the city was substantially that which so much struck the sixteenth-century missionaries when they spoke with such enthusiasm of Meaco (*i.e., miyako,* the capital).

A comparison between Kyoto and Florence is almost impossible to avoid. Not only do they have similar connotations in their respective civilizations; there is also a physical resemblance. True, the valley of the Arno between San Domenico and San Miniato is narrower than that of the Kamogawa, but Florence seen from the Viale dei Colli and Kyoto from the Higashi-yama are essentially two seas of houses filling flat valleys between mountains and hills; and, just as Florence has Fiesole, the Poggio Imperiale, Settignano, so Kyoto has Higashi-yama, Saga, and Ohara. Moreover, the economic basis of the two places is similar. In both it is agriculture, for the most part in the hands of old families, and in both a class of artisans is gradually being industrialized. However, the view that lay below me was far less beautiful than that of Florence seen, say, from the Piazzale Michelangelo. In this sea of grey roofs you would search in vain for the counterpart of lines, spaces, and volumes that springs to life from the bridges across the Arno, from the towers, domes, and *campanili;* for the sense of completeness and unity of which the supreme examples are San Gimignano among the cities of the Old World, and New York, the modern San Gimignano, among the cities of the New.

Moreover, going down into Kyoto and walking about the central streets between the Shi-jo and San-jo bridges and the avenues of Imadegawa, it is easy to feel a great sense of disappointment. In contrast to the cities of

Europe, which offer new perspectives at every turn, Kyoto, like every other Japanese town, consists of broad, anonymous streets intersecting at right-angles and flanked by neat, often attractive-looking, houses, all similar except when they are interrupted by ugly modern buildings of no style at all. True, at Kyoto everything is better cared-for, less brazenly utilitarian, than in other Japanese towns, and near some of the temples (Higashi and Nishi Hongan-ji), in certain streets (Teramachi, Ponto-cho), and in the parks surrounding the Imperial Palaces, there are views which are sometimes impressive, sometimes pleasing and full of fascination, and sometimes truly magnificent; nevertheless a superficial drive through the city rouses no particular enthusiasm.

In spite of that Kyoto has a wealth of beauty which is not surpassed anywhere in the world. Once more we touch on one of the fundamental differences between Europe and the Far East. Florence is western beauty displayed for all to see; Kyoto is eastern; its beauty is concealed, a secret to be wrested from it little by little. True, you can spend a month at Florence, visiting churches, galleries, villas, *palazzi;* but you can also claim to be able to see it in a single afternoon, from the surrounding hills, the tops of its towers, from its streets, squares, bridges. It is characteristic that the Higashi-yama ('Eastern Mount'), the Fiesole of Kyoto, has no street or viewpoint from which the city can be seen as a whole; the point to which I climbed was a woodman's path, full of slippery slopes and covered with pine-needles. The idea of a view is entirely western and entirely un-Japanese. What bad taste, what barbarism, what childishness, to want to see everything all at once! Hence the things that matter at Kyoto are tucked away in little valleys, in green alcoves between the folds of the hills. Its beauties do not present themselves, but have to be sought out.

FOSCO MARAINI
Meeting with Japan, 1960

WEEPING CHERRIES, GOLDEN TEMPLE

Although written during World War II, Junichiro Tanizaki's The Makioka Sisters *deliberately turns its back upon the cataclysmic events of those years, focusing instead upon the serenity and order of the previous decade. "I tried to limit myself to what was attractive," the author later observed, and his saga of the Makiokas, a wealthy upper-class merchant family from Osaka, consciously evokes the sentiments of a bygone era. Nevertheless, the following excerpt, which recounts the family's annual pilgrimage to Kyoto at the peak of the brief cherry-blossom season, is tinged with sadness. For Sachiko, eldest of the sisters, the fragility of the blooms is a reminder of the transience of happiness. For Tanizaki, the intrusion of Western customs and dress represents the first gust of what he calls "the enveloping storm."*

All these hundreds of years, from the days of the oldest poetry collections, there have been poems about cherry blossoms. The ancients waited for cherry blossoms, grieved when they were gone, and lamented their passing in countless poems. How very ordinary the poems had seemed to Sachiko when she read them as a girl, but now she knew, as well as one could know, that grieving over fallen cherry blossoms was more than a fad or a convention. The family — Sachiko, her husband and daughter, her two younger sisters — had for some years now been going to Kyoto in the spring to see the cherry blossoms. The excursion had become a fixed annual observance. Sometimes Teinosuke

153

or Etsuko would be missing because of work or school, but at least the three sisters were always together. For Sachiko there was, besides pleasant sorrow for the cherry blossoms, sorrow for her sisters and the passing of their youth. She wondered whether each excursion might not be her last with Yukiko, at least. And her sisters seemed to feel much the same emotions. Not as fond of cherry blossoms as Sachiko, they still took great pleasure in the outing. Long before — at the time of the Spring Festival in Nara, early in March — they began waiting for it, and planning what they would wear.

As the season approached, there would be reports on when the cherries were likely to be in full bloom. They had to pick a week-end, for the convenience of Etsuko and Teinosuke, and they all had the anxiety of the ancients over the weather, anxiety which had once seemed to Sachiko merely conventional. With each breeze and each shower their concern for the cherries would grow. There were cherries enough around the Ashiya house, and cherries to be seen from the window of the train into Osaka, and there was no need to go all the way to Kyoto; but Sachiko had firm views on what was best. When it came to sea bream, only Akashi bream seemed worth eating, and she felt that she had not seen the cherry blossoms at all unless she went to Kyoto. Teinosuke had rebelled the year before and taken them instead to the Brocade Bridge; but Sachiko had been restless afterwards, as though she had forgotten something. She complained that spring did not feel like spring, and finally took Teinosuke off to Kyoto in time for the late cherries at Omuro. The annual procedure was fixed: they arrived in Kyoto on Saturday afternoon, had an early dinner at the Gourd Restaurant, and, after the spring dances, which they never missed, saw the Gion cherries by lantern light. On Sunday morning they went to the western suburbs. After lunch by the river at Storm Hill, they returned to the city in time to see the weeping cherries in the Heian Shrine; and with that, whether or not Teinosuke and Sachiko stayed on another night by themselves, the outing proper was finished.

The cherries in the Heian Shrine were left to the last because they, of all the cherries in Kyoto, were the most beautiful. Now that the great weeping cherry in Gion was dying and its blossoms were growing paler each year, what was left to stand for the Kyoto spring if not the cherries in the Heian Shrine? And so, coming back from the western suburbs on the afternoon of the second day, and picking that moment of regret when the spring sun was about to set, they would pause, a little tired, under the trailing branches, and look fondly at each tree — on around the lake, by the approach to a bridge, by a bend in the path, under the eaves of the gallery. And, until the cherries came the following year, they could close their eyes and see again the color and line of a trailing branch.

Choosing a week-end in mid-April, they set out. Etsuko, who put on a kimono scarcely ten times a year, and would have been uncomfortable in any case, was wearing a kimono a little too small for her. An intent expression on her holiday face (it was touched up very slightly with cosmetics), she concentrated on keeping her sandals from slipping off and her kimono from coming open. At dinner, a bare knee finally slipped through. She was clearly more at home in Western clothes. She still had her own childish way of holding chopsticks, moreover, and the kimono sleeve seemed to get in her way. When a particularly slippery vegetable shot from the chopsticks, slithered across the veranda, and came to rest in the moss outside, she was as pleased as the rest. The year's expedition was off to a good start.

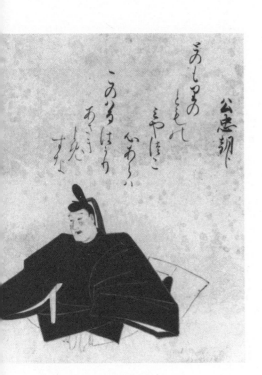

The next morning they strolled first of all along the banks of Hirosawa Pond. Teinosuke took a picture with his Leica of the four of them — Sachiko, Etsuko, Yukiko, and Taeko — lined up in that order under a cherry tree whose branches trailed off into the water. They had a happy memory of the spot: one spring, as they had been walking along the pond, a gentleman had asked them most politely if he might take their picture. Writing down their address, he promised to send prints if the snapshots turned out well; and among the prints that arrived some ten days later was a truly remarkable one. Sachiko and Etsuko, turned away from the camera, were looking out over the rippled surface of the lake from under this same cherry tree, and the two rapt figures, mother and daughter, with cherry petals falling on the gay kimono of the little girl, seemed the very incarnation of regret for the passing of spring. Ever since, they had made it a point to stand under the same tree and look out over the pond, and have their picture taken. Sachiko knew too that in the hedge that lined the path there would be a camellia loaded with crimson blossoms. She never forgot to look for it.

They climbed the embankment of Osawa Pond for a brief look at the cherries there, and went on past the temple gates — the Temple of the Great Awakening, the Temple of Clean Coolness, the Temple of the Heavenly Dragon — to arrive at the Bridge of the Passing Moon, beyond which, rising from the river, was Storm Hill with its cherry blossoms. At Storm Hill there were always throngs of Korean women in the plain yet richly dyed clothes of their peninsula, bringing a touch of the exotic and cosmopolitan to spring in the old capital. This year too, under the cherry trees along the river, they were gathered in twos and threes and fives, some of them stirred by the cherry-blossom saké to a rather unladylike ebullience. . . .

A chilly wind had come up by the time they passed the Nonomiya, the Shrine in the Fields, where in ancient times court maidens retired for purification before leaving to become Shrine Virgins at Ise. At the Enrian Hermitage a shower of cherry petals was falling, to decorate their kimono sleeves. Again they walked through the Temple of Clean Coolness, and, taking a train, arrived back at the Bridge of the Passing Moon yet a third time. After a rest they hailed a cab and drove to the Heian Shrine.

Those weeping cherries just beyond the gallery to the left as one steps inside the gate and faces the main hall — those cherries said to be famous even abroad — how would they be this year? Was it perhaps already too late? Always they stepped through the gallery with a strange rising of the heart, but the five of them cried out as one when they saw that cloud of pink spread across the late-afternoon sky.

It was the climax of the pilgrimage, the moment treasured through a whole year. All was well, they had come again to the cherries in full bloom. There was a feeling of relief, and a hope that next year they might be as fortunate, and for Sachiko, at least, the thought that even if she herself stood here next year, Yukiko might be married and far away. The flowers would come again, but Yukiko would not. It was a saddening thought, and yet it contained almost a prayer that, for Yukiko's sake, she might indeed no longer be with them. Sachiko had stood under these same trees with these same emotions the year before and the year before that, and each time she had found it hard to understand why they should still be together. . . .

One morning some days later, when Teinosuke had left for work and Sachiko was cleaning his study, she noticed a sheet of paper on the desk. In the margin, beside several lines written in the cursive style, was this poem:

>Near Kyoto, on a day in April:
>"The beauties gather in festive dress.
>For the cherries are in bloom,
>At Saga in old Miyako."

Sachiko had been fond of poetry when she was in school, and recently, under the influence of her husband, she had taken to jotting down poems as they came to her. Teinosuke's poem aroused her interest. A verse that she had not been able to finish at the Heian Shrine presently finished itself in her mind:

>Under the falling flowers, at the Heian Shrine:
>"The cherry blossoms that fall
>And leave us to mourn the spring —
>I shall hide them here in my sleeve."

She wrote it beside Teinosuke's verse, and left the paper as she had found it. Teinosuke said nothing when he came home that evening, and Sachiko herself quite forgot her poem. The next morning as she started to clean the study, she found a new verse penned in after hers. Possibly it was a suggested revision.

>"Let me hide at least a petal
>In the sleeve of my flower-viewing robe,
>That I may remember the spring."

>JUNICHIRO TANIZAKI
>*The Makioka Sisters*, 1957

Obsessed by the "unbearable" beauty of Kyoto's famed Golden Pavilion, which he looked upon as a reproof to his own ugliness, an unbalanced student of Zen Buddhism set the frail wooden structure afire in 1950. The mindless destruction of Kinkaku-ji, which many considered the finest of Kyoto's extant structures, scandalized and horrified the Japanese, who lost no time in erecting a facsimile of the razed temple. The incident itself became the subject of a psychological novel by Yukio Mishima, a brilliant young author similarly haunted by his own imperfection. Mishima's grotesque ritual suicide in 1970 created another scandal of national scope — and cast a new light on fictional passages such as this one from The Temple of the Golden Pavilion.

It is no exaggeration to say that the first real problem I faced in my life was that of beauty. My father was only a simple country priest, deficient in vocabulary, and he taught me that "there is nothing on this earth so beautiful as the Golden Temple." At the thought that beauty should already have come into this world unknown to me, I could not help feeling a certain uneasiness and irritation. If beauty really did exist there, it meant that my own existence was a thing estranged from beauty.

But for me the Golden Temple was never simply an idea. The mountains blocked it from my sight, yet, if I should want to see it, the temple was always there for me to go and see. Beauty was thus an object that one could touch with one's fingers, that could be clearly reflected in one's eyes. I knew and I believed that, amid all the changes of the world, the Golden Temple remained there safe and immutable.

There were times when I thought of the Golden Temple as being like a small, delicate piece of workmanship that I could put in my hands; there were times, also, when I thought of it as a huge, monstrous cathedral that soared up endlessly into the sky. Being a young boy, I could not think of beauty as being neither small nor large, but a thing of moderation. So when I saw small, dew-drenched summer flowers that seemed to emit a vague light, they seemed to me as beautiful as the Golden Temple. Again, when the gloomy, thunder-packed clouds stood boldly on the other side of the hills, with only the edges shining in gold, their magnificence reminded me of the Golden Temple. Finally it came about that even when I saw a beautiful face, the simile would spring into my mind: "lovely as the Golden Temple."

It was a sad journey. The Maizuru-line trains went from West Maizuru to Kyoto by way of Ayabe and stopped at all the small stations like Makura and Uesugi. The carriage was dirty, and when we reached the Hozu Ravine and began to go through one tunnel after another, the smoke poured in mercilessly and made Father cough again and again. . . .

I looked out of the window at the cloudy, leaden spring sky. I looked at the robe that Father wore over his civilian uniform, and at the breast of a ruddy young petty officer, which seemed to leap up along his row of gilt buttons. I felt as if I were situated between the two men. . . .

I tried to look after my father when he coughed. Now and then I caught sight of the Hozu River outside the window. It was a dark-blue, almost heavy color, like the copper sulfate used in chemistry experiments. Each time that the train emerged from a tunnel, the Hozu Ravine would appear either some . . . distance from the tracks or unexpectedly close at hand. . . .

I did not feel that this ancient sooty train was really bound for the city. I felt that it was headed for the station of death. Once this thought had come into my mind, the smoke that filled our carriage each time that we passed through a tunnel had the smell of the crematorium.

Despite it all, when finally I stood before the Somon Gate of the Rokuonji, my heart was throbbing. Now I was to see one of the most beautiful things in the world.

The sun was beginning to go down and the hills were veiled in mist. Several other visitors were passing through the gate at about the same time as Father and I. On the left of the gate stood the belfry, surrounded by a cluster of plum trees, which were still in bloom.

A great oak tree grew in front of the Main Hall. Father stood in the entrance and asked for admission. The Superior sent a message that he was busy with a visitor and asked us if he would wait for a while.

"Let's use this time to go round and look at the Golden Temple," said Father.

Father evidently wanted to show me that he exerted some influence in this place and he tried to go through the visitors' entrance without paying the admission fee. But both the man who sold tickets and religious charms and the ticket collector at the gate had changed since the time, some ten years earlier, when Father used to come often to the temple.

"Next time I come," said Father with a chilly expression, "I suppose they'll have changed again."

But I felt that Father no longer really believed in this "next time."

I hurried ahead of Father, almost running. I was deliberately acting like a cheerful young boy. (It was only at such times — only when I put on a deliberate performance — that there was anything boyish about me.) Then the Golden Temple, about which I had dreamed so much, displayed its entire form to me most disappointingly.

I stood by the edge of the Kyoko Pond, and on the other side of the water the Golden Temple revealed its façade in the declining sun. The Sosei was half hidden farther to the left. The Golden Temple cast a perfect shadow on the surface of the pond, where the duckweed and the leaves from water plants were floating. The shadow was more beautiful than the building itself. The setting sun was making the reflection of the water wave to and fro on the back of the eaves of all three stories. Compared to the surrounding light, the reflection of the back of the eaves was too dazzling and clear; the Golden Temple gave me the impression that it was proudly bending itself back.

"Well, what do you think?" said Father. "It's beautiful, isn't it? The first story is called the Housi-in, the second is the Choondo, and the third is the Kukyocho." Father placed his ill, emaciated hand on my shoulder.

I changed my angle of vision a few times and bent my head in various directions. But the temple aroused no emotion within me. It was merely a small, dark, old, three-storied building. The phoenix on top of the roof looked like a crow that had alighted there for a rest. Not only did the building fail to strike me as beautiful, but I even had a sense of disharmony and restlessness. Could beauty, I wondered, be as unbeautiful a thing as this?

If I had been a modest, studious boy, I should have regretted my own deficiency in aesthetic appreciation before becoming so quickly discouraged as I did. But the pain of having been deceived by something of which I had expected so much robbed me of all other considerations.

It occurred to me that the Golden Temple might have adopted some disguise to hide its true beauty. Was it not possible that, in order to protect itself from people, the beauty deceived those who observed it? I had to approach the Golden Temple closer; I had to remove the obstacles that seemed ugly to my eyes; I had to examine it all, detail by detail, and with these eyes of mine perceive the essence of its beauty. Inasmuch as I believed only in the beauty that one can see with one's eyes, my attitude at the time was quite natural.

With a respectful air Father now led me up to the open corridor of the Hosui-in. First I looked at the skillfully executed model of the Golden Temple that rested in a glass case. This model pleased me. It was closer to the Golden Temple of my dreams. Observing this perfect little image of the Golden Temple within the great temple itself, I was reminded of the endless series of correspondences that arise when a small universe is placed in a large universe and a smaller one in turn placed inside the small universe. For the first time I could dream. Of the small, but perfect Golden Temple which was even smaller than this model; and of the Golden Temple which was infinitely greater than the real building — so great, indeed, that it almost enveloped the world.

I did not, however, remain standing indefinitely before the model. Next Father led me to the wooden statue of Yoshimitsu, which was famous as a National Treasure. The statue was known as the Rokuoninden-Michiyoshi, after the name that Yoshimitsu adopted when he took the tonsure.

This, too, struck me as being nothing but an old, sooty image and I could sense no beauty in it. Next we went up to the Choondo on the second story and looked at the painting on the ceiling, attributed to Kano Masanobu, which depicted angels playing music. On the third story, the Kukyocho, I saw the pathetic remains of the gold leaf that had originally covered all the interior. I could find no beauty in any of this.

I leaned against the slender railing and looked down absently at the pond, on which the evening sun was shining. The surface of the water looked like a mirror, like an ancient patinated copper mirror; and the shadow of the Golden Temple fell directly on this surface. The evening sky was reflected in the water, far beneath the water plants and the duckweed. This sky was different from the one above our heads. It was clear and filled with a serene light; from underneath and from within, it entirely swallowed up this earthly world of ours, and the Golden Temple sank into it like a great anchor of pure gold that has become entirely black with rust.

YUKIO MISHIMA
The Temple of the Golden Pavilion, 1959

THE PAST REVIVED

In September of 1968, American historian John Whitney Hall returned to Kyoto, his childhood home, to address a special conference on the relationship between Japanese and Western art. His speech, which begins in reverie and ends in exhortation, explores — and ultimately decries — the impact that a century of rapid Westernization has had on traditional Japanese art and on the country's sense of historical identity.

It is with a deep sense of nostalgia, . . . that I stand before you this morning. Kyoto is the city of my youth. I lived here in the days before the tower. I have known Hieizan [Mount Hiei] in all its many moods, in fact I have climbed it on foot before the *doraivuwei* [driveways] marred its flanks or the parking lot was carved out of the forest by the side of Komponchûdô. I should like to boast that I have known the "old" Kyoto. But each generation, it would seem, has observed the passing of this city's former glories, and KAMO-NO Chômei has preceded me in the lament for a better Kyoto. From Kamakura times to now, change is the essence of history. "The flow of the river is ceaseless and its water is never the same."

But if KAMO-NO Chômei was saddened by the decay of a Kyoto he once admired, what of us who have seen the transformation of the last hundred years? Has not the last century, which has brought Japan to its pinnacle of world prominence, been more ruinous to the old Kyoto than the entire eleven hundred years which preceded it? Is it not deeply significant that the emperor abandoned Kyoto in 1869 for Tokyo where he eventually took up his residence in a Western style palace? The currents of change in the last hundred years have placed Kyoto in double jeopardy. For the country of which it was once the capital has been swept by both the modernizing currents of technological change, and by powerful winds of influence from an alien civilization. The last hundred years have been hard on Kyoto and what it once stood for. And as a Sôseki or a TANIZAKI have expressed so eloquently in their works, this has been the source of deep disturbance for the artist and the writer in Japan. The question which they seem to ask is in our hearts as well. Can Kyoto be saved, and with it the cultural values that it once stood for? But should Kyoto be saved? There are many in Japan who pay this city the supreme slight of profound indifference, and the guiding spirit of Kyoto itself seems bent on atonement for having escaped untouched from the last war by a continuous act of self-destruction. . . .

What is to become of Kyoto beyond this the hundredth year since the Restoration — this city which increasingly illustrates the visual and functional confusion between a Japanese way, which it carries off so superbly, and an international way, which it wears so awkwardly? Kyoto more than Tokyo forces upon us an awareness of the conflicts and tensions which still can be found in Japanese life, posing constantly the question of where Japan's historical past fits into its modern present. What is Kyoto to modern Japan? Has it not become a relic, simply a pre-"Meiji *mura*" [village] on a gigantic scale? Is not Kyoto ultimately doomed, like so much of traditional life, to be bypassed or to succumb to the glacial advance of a homogeneous international style? Is it not destined in the end to be raised inert and detached like a Nubian monument above the rising waters of "progress."

Not that there is anything fundamentally wrong with inert preservation as such. It is admittedly a necessary first step. And the Japanese nation should be extremely gratified by the remarkable efforts which have been made to preserve its historic monuments, its art forms, and its craft techniques. Museums whether filled with objects or living persons (such as Imbe-yaki potters or Bunraku puppeteers) are essential to the survival of traditions. What is at issue, rather, is how traditions can inform the present? How they can continue as living forces in the present.

The fact is, of course, that we have in our midst, among the participants in this conference, men who begun to exemplify in their own creative works the answer to this question. And it is remarkable how similarly these men arrived at their powers of conscious interplay between Japanese tradition and the wider world audience. In none of the works of architecture, literature, drama, or music which we have admired was the simple act of preservation or imitation sufficient. Something else was required and that is the creative use through remembrance, or more often rediscovery, of meaning in a traditional form or mode. Moreover this creative act has been preceded by a sense of self-confidence which transcended both the act of mastery of a new and universal technique and the return to some newly discovered meaning in a traditional genre. It is dependent in other words on a degree of self-discovery, or, what I would like to call, a sense of historical identity.

This special quality which I refer to is required not simply by the artist but at large within the entire society. And it is the quality which Kyoto must have if it is to remain alive in the years ahead....

The key is rediscovery. It is not sufficient simply that we can go to Ryô-anji and sit, and marvel, without knowing why. We must unlock the mystery of the genius of that work of art in terms that hold meaning for us today. Kyoto is doomed to Museum-like existence as long as it is content to stand at its entrances and fatten itself off the fees it collects from its tourist visitors. ... The prospect of continual flight before the onrush of the Kanko [tourist] bus is frightening. No — flight is not the answer. Kyoto must stand its ground and defend itself. But to do this Kyoto must know itself sufficiently so that it can protect its essence rather than its exterior — its spirit not just its monuments. Moreover it must know what that essence is and it must be able to prove to its own people and to the world that it is not simply age that makes monuments worth viewing, rather that these monuments are repositories of certain living values which are needed in the modern world.

JOHN WHITNEY HALL
Speech delivered in Kyoto, 1968

REFERENCE

Chronology of Japanese History

Entries in boldface refer to Kyoto.

c. 660 B.C.	Accession of Jimmu Tennō, Japan's quasi-legendary first emperor
A.D. 57	First Japanese envoys reach the Chinese court
552	Traditional date assigned to the introduction of Buddhism from mainland China
607	Prince Regent Shōtoku sends first major embassy to mainland China
645–50	Taika ("Great Change") Reform
702	Taihō Code establishes strong central government and national system of tax collection
710	Nara becomes Japan's first permanent capital
712	Compilation of the nation's first official history
752	Dedication of the Great Buddha of Tōdai-ji, Nara
781	Coronation of Japan's fiftieth emperor, Kammu
784	Kammu abandons Nara, moves capital to Nagaoka
794	**Kyoto becomes Japan's third imperial capital**
797	**Earthquake badly damages the new capital**
800	**Kammu inspects his new palace and tours grounds of Shinsen-en, a thirty-three-acre pleasure garden surrounding the royal residence**
806	Priest Kūkai founds Shingon Sect of Buddhism
808	**Plague and famine throughout the capital**
812	Final subjugation of the Ainu in north Honshu
838	Last Japanese embassy to T'ang dynasty China
858	Fujiwara clan assumes control of the government
876	**Daigoku-den, principal hall of state of imperial palace, leveled by a flash fire**
941	Fujiwara clansmen, led by Sumitomo, stage a brief rising in western Honshu before being subdued
951	**Five-tiered pagoda of Daigo-ji constructed**
960	**Major fire reduces half of Kyoto to ashes**
c. 1002	Sei Shōnagon composes *The Pillow Book,* an intimate diary of life at the Heian court
c. 1008	*The Tale of Genji* written by Lady Murasaki
1058	**Disastrous fire consumes entire imperial palace, sparing only the southern gate and a tower**
1062	Minamoto no Yoriyoshi subdues Abe rebellion in northern Honshu after a twelve-year campaign
1068	Emperor Go-Sanjo visits the Phoenix Hall at Byōdō-in, a country villa built by Fujiwara no Yorimichi
1072	**Go-Sanjo abdicates after dedicating the recently rebuilt imperial enclosure**
1160–85	Gempei War between Taira and Minamoto clans
1160	Taira no Kiyomori emerges as undisputed leader of Japan after bloody suppression of Minamoto
1175	Introduction of the Jōdō, or Pure Land, Sect of Buddhism by Hōnen
1177	**Wind-driven fire gluts central Kyoto**
1180	Kiyomori, unnerved by an attempted coup, briefly moves his entire government to Fukuhara
1183	**Last of the Taira driven from Kyoto by Minamoto no Yoshinaka's army**
1185	Final battle of Gempei War, an epic sea duel, fought at Dan-no-ura; Minamoto victorious
c. 1200	Priest Eisai establishes Kennin-ji, first Zen Buddhist temple in Kyoto
1221	Emperor Go-Toba attempts foredoomed coup against Minamoto military administration at Kamakura; rising rapidly suppressed, and many estates seized; end of aristocratic power
1257	Earthquake does extensive damage to Kamakura
1274	First Mongol invasion of Kyushu
1281	Second Mongol invasion; Kublai Khan's armada scattered by *kamikaze,* "divine winds"
1333	Kamakura captured by Emperor Go-Daigo
1337	Go-Daigo banished to Yoshino
1342	*Tenryū-ji-bune* sails for China, inaugurating a new era of profitable trade with the mainland
1378	**Ashikaga Yoshimitsu builds the Hana-no-gosho, or Palace of Flowers, in Muromachi quarter of Kyoto**
1408	Yoshimitsu dies; **his Golden Pavilion is converted, at his behest, into a Zen temple**
1449	**Plague sweeps Kyoto, killing 1,000 persons a day**
1467–77	**Onin War; Kyoto laid waste by opposing armies**
1483	**Ashikaga Yoshimasa completes the Silver Pavilion**
c. 1500	**Sōami lays out the first rock garden at Ryōan-ji**
1536	**Monks of Enryaku-ji raze all Nichiren temples in the capital and its environs**
1549	Arrival of Francis Xavier in Kyushu
1573	Oda Nobunaga, first of Japan's "three heroes," brings century of strife to an end
1582	Nobunaga assassinated; Toyotomi Hideyoshi, one of his trusted lieutenants, succeeds him

162

1586	**Hideyoshi constructs a new palace, the Juraku-dai, on the site of Kammu's first residence**
1587	Edict proscribing Christian worship promulgated
1598	Second Japanese invasion of the mainland ends abruptly following the death of Hideyoshi
1600	Battle of Sekigahara; Tokugawa Ieyasu routs the combined forces of his feudal opponents
1602	**Construction of Nijo Castle begins**
1603	Ieyasu assumes office of shogun, moves Tokugawa administrative headquarters east to Edo
1606	**Hideyoshi's widow founds Kōdai-ji in his honor**
1614–15	Siege of Osaka Castle; Ieyasu extinguishes the Toyotomi line and assumes full control of state
1622–23	Period of greatest Christian martyrdoms
1626	Emperor received at Katsura Detached Palace
1633	**Tokugawa Iemitsu underwrites major renovation of Kiyomizu-dera, Kyoto's oldest temple**
1638	Christian uprising at Shimabara suppressed
1655	**Shūgaku-in Detached Palace completed**
1662	Earthquake destroys Hideyoshi's Great Buddha at Hōkō-ji; image melted down for coinage
1701	Incident of the forty-seven *rōnin*
1705	**Main hall of Nishi Hongan-ji rebuilt after fire**
1716	Shogun Yoshimune introduces austerity program in an effort to curb inflation, stabilize economy
1749	**Keep of Nijo Castle struck by lightning**
1788	**Great Fire of Temmei, one of the worst in world history, consumes most of central Kyoto, including 1,000 shrines and temples and 183,000 homes**
1792	Imperial Russia sends first envoy to Japan in an effort to establish trade with isolationist regime
1797	British East India Company ships enter Nagasaki harbor for the first time
1825	"No Second Thought" Edict, issued by shogunate, urges Japanese citizens to fire upon all foreigners
1837	Rice riots in Osaka; U.S.S. *Morrison* puts into Edo Bay to repatriate Japanese sailors
1853	Commander Matthew C. Perry's four-ship squadron anchors off Uraga; Americans insist upon meeting the shogun to discuss a trade agreement
1854	Perry returns to Edo Bay to press his demands; tentative agreement signed at Kanazawa
1855	**Old Imperial Palace rebuilt after fire**
1858	U.S. Consul Townsend Harris negotiates first treaty between Tokugawa and any foreign power
1860	Assassination of Ii Naosuke, last of the effective Tokugawa *tairō*, or great councillors
1863	Western powers bombard Kyushu ports in retaliation for Japanese attacks upon foreign nationals; **emperor summons shogun to Kyoto**
1868	**Meiji Emperor crowned in Kyoto;** shogunate abolished; imperial capital moved to Edo, which is renamed Tokyo, or "Eastern Capital"
1869	Emperor moves to shogunal castle in Tokyo
1872	Introduction of universal conscription strips samurai of their hereditary rank and income
1874	"Opening" of Korea by Japanese Imperial Army
1889	Promulgation of Japan's first constitution
1894–95	First Sino-Japanese War
1904–05	Russo-Japanese War
1915	**Taishō Emperor crowned at Nijo Castle**
1920	Japan helps found the League of Nations
1928	Japan ratifies the Kellogg-Briand Pact renouncing war; first general elections
1930	Over violent popular objections, government signs London Treaty limiting size of Japan's navy
1931	"Manchurian Incident"; Imperial Army establishes puppet state of Manchukuo
1933	Japan withdraws from League of Nations
1937	Border incident leads to "holy war" against China
1939	**Emperor cedes Nijo Castle to the city of Kyoto, which opens the complex to the public for the first time**
1940	Government signs treaty with the Axis powers; ABCD Embargo cuts oil imports 90 per cent
1941	Japanese aerial attack on U.S. military installation at Pearl Harbor
1942	Imperial Army captures Philippines, Hong Kong, Singapore, and Indonesia; Battle of Midway
1945	Systematic firebombing of major Japanese cities; **Kyoto, removed from list of targets, suffers little damage;** A-bombs dropped on Hiroshima and Nagasaki
1945–48	**Artisans of Kyoto produce goods for export to foreign markets during occupation**
1970	**Kyoto's tourist traffic tops 30 million visitors per year; authorities grapple with pollution problems**

Guide to Japan's Ancient Capital

The Japanese penchant for understatement is reflected in the sobriquet they have assigned to Kyoto: "City of a Thousand Shrines." In actuality, there are more than twice that many hallowed sites in the ancient imperial capital—and as a result any visitor to modern Kyoto is immediately confronted with the unhappy task of reducing this embarrassment of cultural riches to manageable dimensions.

Of necessity, then, any tour of Kyoto is highly selective and idiosyncratic, reflecting individual tastes and time limitations. The most sensible approach to the city and its environs might be a geographical one, since Shinto shrines, Buddhist temples, shogunal palaces, and imperial villas are to be found in every quarter. Within that framework, however, the most rewarding tours are generally the least structured, for the enduring charm of Kyoto lies in its blend of the established and the unexpected, the touted and the unheralded. Visitors who cleave to the prescribed tourist routes miss the beauty of the area's serene and unspoiled country temples—whereas those who shy from the trafficked path forsake the very temples and gardens that originally secured and today uphold Kyoto's reputation.

There are, in fact, almost as many opinions on how to tour Kyoto as there are visitors each year—and that figure now exceeds 33 million. Some argue that the ancient city is at its loveliest in the spring, when cherry blossoms cloud the hills and azaleas dye the ground. Others insist that the crimson tracery of the region's famous maples achieves a superior effect in the fall. Purists contend, however, that foliage distracts from the real beauty of Kyoto—and they therefore recommend the muffled austerity of the winter months.

In short, a case can be made for any quarter in any season, and consequently the abbreviated guide that follows (keyed to the seven sections, A–G, on the map opposite) is intended to serve as only the most tentative sort of introduction:

Section A

Kyoto's major palaces range to either side of a broad east-west thoroughfare that was laid out by the city's founder, the emperor Kammu, in A.D. 794. Near its eastern end stands the **Heian Shrine.** This scaled-down facsimile of Kammu's original palace was erected in 1894 to celebrate the eleven-hundredth anniversary of Kyoto's founding.

Brilliantly colored and absolutely symmetrical in design, the Heian Shrine reveals the influence that China exerted upon ninth-century Japan—an influence that was very much in abeyance by the time the **Old Imperial Palace** was constructed. The utterly unadorned exterior of this royal residence reflects the preference for simplicity of line and economy of detail that are the hallmarks of Japanese imperial architecture.

Nijo Castle, on the other hand, displays the fondness for opulent decor and vivid polychrome embellishment that is properly associated with the Tokugawa shoguns, the feudal lords who ruled Japan from 1600 until the restoration of 1868. More palace than castle, Nijo conveys the arrogance and power of its builders, who felt little need to fortify their principal residence in Kyoto against a cowed and subservient populace. Within Nijo's broad moats and sloping ramparts stands a one-story wooden structure of surprising elegance and fragility. Its exposed wooden surfaces are entirely covered with brilliantly colored carvings in high relief, and its inner partitions comprise a gilded gallery of seventeenth-century art works.

Section B

Nanzen-ji, one of the oldest centers of Zen Buddhism in Japan, lies almost due east of Nijo in the foothills of Higashiyama, Kyoto's Eastern Hills. This labyrinthine complex includes several garden restaurants in which simple meals are served on raised, poolside platforms.

No such amenities exist at **Kiyomizu-dera,** which nonetheless remains the most popular structure in the entire city. It is said that the temple's timbers came from the old imperial palace at Nagaoka, which was dismantled when that city was abandoned in favor of Kyoto at the end of the eighth century. In any event, Kiyomizu-dera is unquestionably the oldest building in the city and one of the most heavily visited. Its great cantilevered viewing platform overlooks the entire Kyoto valley, a panorama that is justly celebrated as one of the most spectacular in the nation.

Equally famous—and as a result equally crowded during the height of the tourist season—is the Hall of Thirty-three Bays, **Sanjūsangendō.** This ill-lit, barnlike structure, four hundred feet in length, houses an eight-foot-high statue of Kannon, the goddess of mercy, carved by the noted twelfth-century sculptor Tankei. The temple's fame rests not upon Tankei's central Kannon, however, but upon the smaller images of the goddess created by the master sculptor's followers. One thousand and one in number, these gilded images stand in serried serenity the length of the hall.

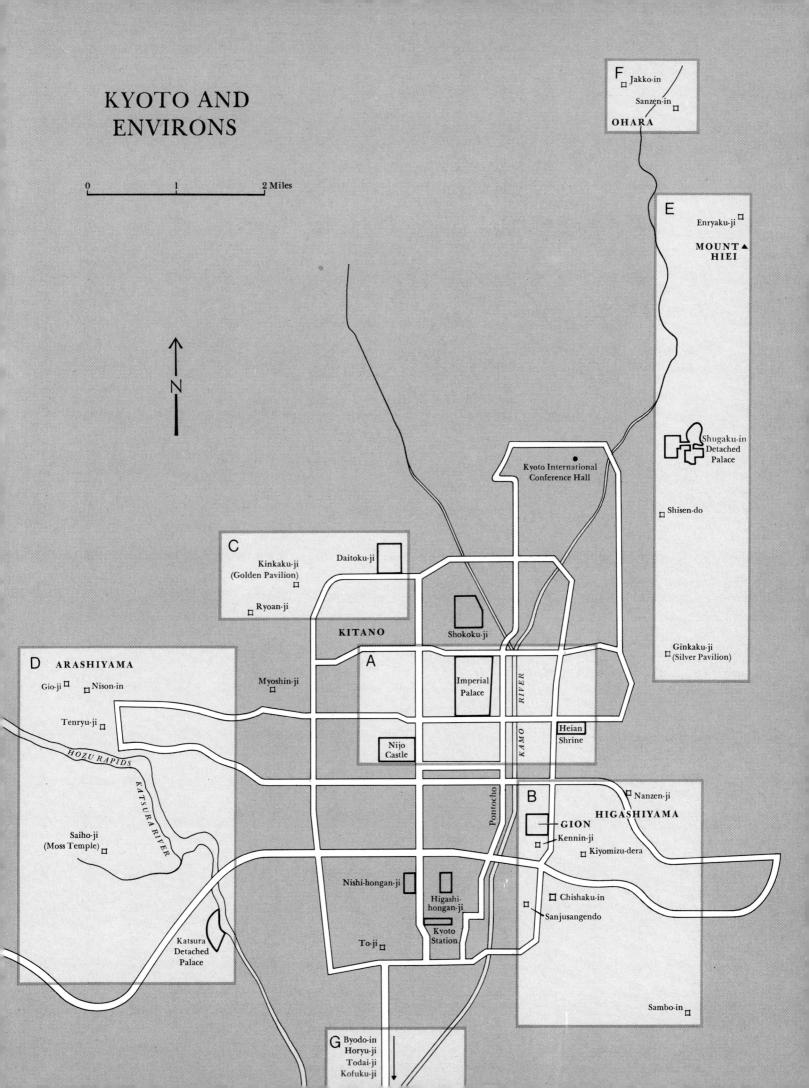

KYOTO AND ENVIRONS

0   1   2 Miles

N

F □ Jakko-in
        Sanzen-in □
OHARA

E   Enryaku-ji □

   MOUNT ▲
   HIEI

                    Shugaku-in
                    Detached
                    Palace

Kyoto International
Conference Hall ●

                    □ Shisen-do

C   Daitoku-ji
   Kinkaku-ji
   (Golden Pavilion)

        □ Ryoan-ji
                      Shokoku-ji
                                        Ginkaku-ji □
   KITANO   (Silver Pavilion)

A

D **ARASHIYAMA**
Gio-ji □ □ Nison-in   Myoshin-ji □   Imperial
                                             Palace
                                                      K A M O   R I V E R
Tenryu-ji □   Heian
                                                              Shrine
HOZU RAPIDS
                            Nijo
                            Castle
K A T S U R A   R I V E R   **B**   □ Nanzen-ji

                                                                        HIGASHIYAMA
Saiho-ji
(Moss Temple) □   □ **GION**
                                                      □ Kennin-ji
                                                              □ Kiyomizu-dera
                                                      Pontocho
                        Nishi-hongan-ji □
                                          Higashi-   □ Chishaku-in
Katsura   hongan-ji □
Detached   Sanjusangendo
Palace   To-ji □   Kyoto
                                   Station
                                                                        Sambo-in □

G □ Byodo-in
     Horyu-ji
     Todai-ji
     Kofuku-ji

The contrast between Sanjūsangendō and the nearby temple of **Chishaku-in** is dramatic indeed, and the two should really be seen in succession. The hall of the golden Kannons is undeniably impressive, but it lacks both the grace and the intimacy of its immediate neighbor. The gardens of Chishaku-in, a tranquil oasis in the heart of one of Kyoto's busier districts, were purportedly laid out by Sen no Rikyū, the renowned master of tea who was the supreme arbiter of sixteenth-century taste. A small museum on the temple grounds houses a group of painted screens attributed to Hasegawa Tōhaku and said to be the finest surviving examples of Momoyama art.

It is both intriguing and instructive to compare Sen no Rikyū's gardens at Chishaku-in with the gardens of **Sambō-in,** laid out at the behest of Rikyū's foremost patron, the hegemon Toyotomi Hideyoshi. The former gardens are a model of restraint; the latter, an exercise in extravagance. A living testament to Hideyoshi's penchant for the grandiose, Sambō-in is nonetheless one of the most magnificent gardens in a city famed for its gardens.

Section C

Sen no Rikyū is also said to have designed the two-storied main entrance of **Daitoku-ji,** the huge Zen temple that occupies some twenty-seven acres in Kyoto's northern sector, and the tea master is interred on the grounds. Seven of Daitoku-ji's twenty-two lesser temples are open to the public. These range from the disagreeably commercialized Daisen-in, whose gardens by Sōami, Japan's legendary master of landscape gardening, are among the very

finest in the nation; to the tiny, tranquil Ryōgen-in, which also boasts a garden by Sōami and which encloses the smallest rock garden in the city; to the lush and alluring Kōtō-in, with its mossy walkways and ubiquitous floral displays.

West of Daitoku-ji, set in the midst of a densely wooded park, is **Kinkaku-ji,** the world famous Golden Pavilion. For centuries this graceful relic of the Muromachi era was regarded as a near-perfect paradigm of fifteenth-century aesthetics, a glittering, captivating expression of the nation's cultural golden age. Then, in 1950, the frail, three-tiered wooden structure was wantonly destroyed by an unbalanced Zen acolyte. An exact replica was erected on the same site five years later, but this new pavilion lacks the soft patina and unassertive glow of its predecessor.

If the Golden Pavilion is the most readily recognized of Kyoto's temples, **Ryōan-ji** is indisputably the most readily recognized of its gardens. Indeed, the gravel and rock garden of this Zen temple has been called the most instantaneously identifiable man-made landscape in the world. Curiously unaffected by its own notoriety, Ryōan-ji garden remains true to its original conception. Five centuries after its creation by the great Sōami as a three-dimensional embodiment of Zen principles, this enigmatic arrangement of raked gravel and boulders still strikes visitors as being, simultaneously, breathtakingly simple and infinitely complex.

Section D

Katsura Detached Palace, which lies almost due south of Ryōan-ji, creates precisely the opposite impression: its meticulously maintained gardens are

calculated to elicit a controlled and predictable response from all who visit them. The individual effects are almost undetectable, but the cumulative impact is nothing less than sublime. Many consider the grounds surrounding this princely estate the apotheosis of Japanese landscape gardening — a triumphant synthesis of all previous techniques and a perfect expression of aristocratic aesthetics. Astonishingly enough, the entire garden — hillocks, lake, islands — is wholly man-made, rising where rice paddies once stood.

The fame of Katsura's gardens tends to overshadow the importance of the villa itself, a structure whose austerity of line and elegance of detail have led art historians to observe that the designers of the Katsura palace anticipated the best features of the Bauhaus by almost three hundred years. Because it is constructed of bamboo and rice paper, the villa is too frail to withstand heavy tourist traffic, and consequently the interior is closed to the general public. The gardens — which are especially lovely during a spring rain — are open throughout the year.

Visitors to Kyoto are likewise urged to choose a rainy day to tour **Saihō-ji,** the spectacular Moss Temple, whose justly celebrated ground cover assumes a special verdancy at such times. Created by the eminent fourteenth-century Zen priest Musō, the garden at Saihō-ji lies beneath a three-inch-thick blanket of mosses. Some fifty varieties of this velvety plant contribute to the garden's extraordinary range of color and texture.

Musō is also credited with having designed the gardens at **Tenryū-ji,** the huge temple complex situated just above the Hozu Rapids, a popular picnic and boating area north of Saihō-ji. Built with money raised through trade with China, Tenryū-ji has long dominated the Arashiyama district. The temple itself is surrounded by old villas and tiny shops, but its gardens survey the whole of Arashiyama — thus appropriating one of the area's most spectacular vistas.

No tour of Arashiyama should conclude without a visit to one or more of the region's country temples. This group includes **Nison-in,** hidden in a handsome stand of Japanese maples, and tiny **Gio-ji,** perched on a steep hillside in the midst of a bamboo grove.

Section E

Kyoto's most famous example of *shakkei,* or "borrowed scenery" landscaping, is **Shūgaku-in Detached Palace,** which occupies a sprawling site at the foot of Mount Hiei, across the Kyoto valley from Gio-ji. Actually three semidetached clusters of buildings set in separate gardens, the sixty-nine-acre compound boasts one of the most dramatic natural settings in the entire region. A great retaining wall of earth and stone, built in the seventeenth century to create a large artificial pond, screens the upper villa from the town below, creating an illusion of unspoiled wilderness on the northern edge of a modern city of some 1.5 million people.

Equally illusory are the gardens that surround **Ginkaku-ji,** which lies somewhat nearer the center of Kyoto. Dense forests envelop this fifteenth-century villa, which is known as the Silver Pavilion despite the fact that it never received its intended coat of silver leaf. The surrounding gardens, often attributed to Sōami, include peculiarly shaped mounds of white sand that were

designed to throw moonbeams into the pavilion's interior.

The use of white sand for decorative effect is even more pronounced at **Shisen-do,** where raked gravel and severely clipped azaleas are strikingly combined. Built in the early seventeenth century by a poet-recluse, the principal structure is hung with portraits of thirty-six of China's greatest poets, all of them the work of the great Tokugawa-period artist Kanō Tanyu.

Unquestionably the largest and most famous of Kyoto's outlying temples is **Enryaku-ji,** the enormous Buddhist complex atop Mount Hiei. Once the rallying point for militant monks determined to subvert the authority of the crown, Enryaku-ji today attracts visitors bent on viewing all of Kyoto and most of Lake Biwa from the temple's lofty precincts.

Section F

Where Enryaku-ji is sprawling and complex, the temples of Ohara are compact and extremely simple. The minuscule nunnery of **Jakkō-in** is, in fact, the quintessence of country temples — and it is only a shade more secluded than **Sanzen-in,** whose gardens encircle a magnificently preserved Fujiwara-era temple, the Hall of Paradise in Rebirth.

There are, of course, other points of interest in Kyoto: **Tō-ji,** the tallest pagoda in Japan; **Higashi Hongan-ji,** whose mammoth Founder's Hall supports the largest wooden roof in the world; **Myōshin-ji,** with its wealth of Buddhist art treasures. But visitors to the City of a Thousand Shrines may wish to interrupt their exploration for a day-long side trip to Japan's first permanent capital, Nara.

Section G

Any excursion to the south begins at Uji, a hamlet famous for its green tea and for **Byōdō-in,** the phoenix-capped temple that is the supreme architectural achievement of Kyoto's first great imperial age. Less than an hour distant by train is **Hōryū-ji,** a Chinese-style monastery that includes the oldest wooden buildings in the world, erected in the eighth century. Nara itself boasts the famed temples of **Kōfuku-ji** and **Tōdai-ji,** the last of which houses a massive, fifty-three-foot-high Buddha weighing more than a million pounds.

Returning at dusk to Kyoto, the tourist may savor the city's nighttime atmosphere in any of a number of ways and in any of a number of places: from the Eastern Hills, where overlooks along the Higashiyama Drive enable the modern visitor to Kammu's capital to trace the old city's outlines in flickering neon; from Pontocho, the narrow walkway that parallels the Kamo River as it sweeps through the city's center; or from any of the discreetly labeled establishments in Gion, the lantern-hung amusement quarter where Kyoto's renowned *maiko* dancers perform to the sounds of the koto and samisen.

The list is necessarily incomplete, and the descriptions sketchy — but the point is inescapably clear: Kyoto is a trove of incalculable cultural riches and all but endless variety, a city of profound beauty on the one hand and commonplace charm on the other. More, its scenic spots, sacred halls, and revered art treasures are immutable testament to the former imperial capital's monumental contribution to the arts, architecture, and aesthetics — in Japan and in the world.

167

Selected Bibliography

Downs, Ray F., ed., *Japan Yesterday and Today*. New York: Bantam Books, Inc., 1970.

Hall, John Whitney. *Japan from Prehistory to Modern Times*. New York: The Delacorte Press, 1970.

Japan Travel Bureau. *Japan, The Official Guide*. Tokyo: Tourist Industry Bureau, 1963.

Keene, Donald, *Landscapes and Portraits: Appreciations of Japanese Culture*. Tokyo: Kodansha, 1971.

Maraini, Fosco. *Meeting with Japan*. New York: The Viking Press, Inc., 1959.

Morris, Ivan. *The World of the Shining Prince*. Middlesex, England: Penguin Books, Ltd., 1964.

Mosher, Gouverneur. *Kyoto, A Contemplative Guide*. Rutland, Vermont: Charles E. Tuttle, Co., Inc., 1964.

Paine, Robert Treat, and Alexander Sopher. *The Art and Architecture of Japan*. Baltimore: Penguin Books, Inc., 1955.

Ponsonby-Fane, R. A. B. *Kyoto, The Old Capital of Japan*. Kyoto: The Ponsonby Memorial Society, 1956.

Reischauer, Edwin O. *Japan Past and Present*. New York: Alfred A. Knopf, Inc., 1964.

Sansom, G. B. *Japan, A Short Cultural History*. New York: Appleton-Century-Crofts, 1962.

Statler, Oliver. *Japanese Inn*. New York: Random House, Inc., 1961.

———. *The Black Ship Scroll*. Tokyo: John Weatherhill, 1963.

Tamburello, Adolfo. *Monuments of Civilization: Japan*. New York: Grosset & Dunlap, Inc., 1973.

Acknowledgments and Picture Credits

The Editors make grateful acknowledgment for the use of excerpted material from the following works:

Japan, China by Nikos Kazantzakis. Copyright © 1963 by Simon & Schuster, Inc. The excerpt appearing on pages 148–50 is reproduced by permission of Simon & Schuster, Inc.

Meeting With Japan by Fosco Maraini. Copyright © 1959 by Hutchinson and Co. (Publishers) Ltd. The excerpt appearing on pages 152–53 is reproduced by permission of The Viking Press.

Pillow Book of Sei Shonagon. Translated by Ivan Morris. Copyright © 1968 by Ivan Morris. The excerpt appearing on pages 138–39 is reproduced by permission of Columbia University Press.

The Makioka Sisters by Junichiro Tanizaki. Translated by Edward G. Seidensticker. Copyright © 1957 by Alfred A. Knopf, Inc. The excerpt appearing on pages 153–56 is reproduced by permission of Alfred A. Knopf, Inc.

The Silent Traveler in Japan by Chiang Yee. Copyright © 1972 by W. W. Norton & Co., Inc. The excerpt appearing on pages 151–52 is reproduced by permission of W. W. Norton & Co., Inc.

The Temple of the Golden Pavilion by Yukio Mishima. Translated by Ivan Morris. Copyright © 1959 by Alfred A. Knopf, Inc. The excerpt appearing on pages 156–59 is reproduced by permission of Alfred A. Knopf, Inc.

"Traditional Arts and the Japanese Sense of Historical Identity During a Hundred Years of Modern Change" by Professor John Whitney Hall. Lecture delivered on September 30, 1968, at the meeting of "International Round Table on the Relation between Japanese and Western Arts" organized by UNESCO in collaboration with the Japanese National Commission for UNESCO. The excerpt appearing on pages 159–60 is reproduced by permission of the Japanese National Commission for UNESCO.

The Editors would like to express their particular appreciation to Margaret Shepard Bayrd, New York; to Barbara Reid and A. H. Matano of Sekai Bunka, New York; and to Prof. George Elison of Colby College, Waterville, Maine, for their invaluable assistance. In addition, the Editors would like to thank the following organizations and individuals:

Russell Ash, London

Council on International Exchange — Bebe P. Johnson, Irving B. Sanders

Japan House Gallery, New York — Rand Castile, Maryell Semal

Japanese Consulate, New York — Goro Nakasone

Imperial Household Agency, Tokyo — Kiroshi Kojima

Takeshi and Taeko Kawase, Tokyo

Bernard Krisher, Tokyo

Ministry of Foreign Affairs, Tokyo — Takahisa Sasaki

Barbara Nagelsmith, Paris

Michio and Kazuko Nakano, Yokohama

National Museum, Tokyo — Shigetaka Kaneko

Seattle Art Museum — Henry Trubner

Lynn Seiffer, New York

Hiroko Suzuki, Tokyo

The title or description of each picture appears after the page number (boldface), followed by its location. Photographic credits appear in parentheses. The following abbreviations are used:

(EB) — (Edwin Bayrd)
NM,T — National Museum, Tokyo
SAM — Eugene Fuller Memorial Collection, Seattle Art Museum
(SB) — Sekai Bunka, Tokyo and New York

ENDPAPERS *Scenes In and Around Kyoto,* screen, 17th century. Okayama Art Museum (SB) HALF TITLE Symbol by Jay J. Smith Studio FRONTISPIECE Fushimi Inari, Kyoto. (Sekai Bunka) **9** Kakiemon ware, Edo period. Freer Gallery of Art, Washington **10–11** Daisen-in gardens, Kyoto. (Nancy Crampton) **12–13** *Uji Bridge,* screen, 16th century. NM,T (SB)

CHAPTER I **15** Bronze sword fitting, 6th century. SAM **16** Bowl, Jomon period. Tohoku University, Miyagi (SB) **17** Vessel, Jomon period. Scientific Museum, Nagaoka City (SB) **18** top, Pot, Yayoi period. NM,T (SB); bottom, House, *haniwa.* (SB) **18–19** Two figures from Konanmura, Saitama, *haniwa.* NM,T (SB) **19** Horse, *haniwa.* Board of Education of Katsuta City, Ibaragii (SB) **20** Buddhist altar fitting from the Horyu-ji, Nara, 8th century. NM,T (SB) **22** Kondo and Five-storied Pagoda, Horyu-ji, Nara. (Japan National Tourist Office) **23** Portrait of Prince Regent Shotoku and two sons, 7th century. Imperial Household Collection, Kyoto (SB) **24** Daibutsu-den, Todai-ji, Nara (Sekai Bunka) **25** Great Buddha of Daibutsu-den, Todai-ji, Nara (Japan National Tourist Office) **26** top, Impression of seal given by Chinese Emperor Kuang-wu to Japanese envoy, A.D. 57. Copy: NM,T (SB); bottom, *Chinese Priests in Japan,* scroll, 7–8th century. Toshodai-ji, Nara (SB) **27** Bronze temple fitting, Heian period. Chuson-ji, Iwate Prefecture (SB) **28** Map by Francis & Shaw, Inc. **31** Shinsen-en. (EB)

CHAPTER II **33** Gilt wood apsaras, late Heian period. SAM **34–35** Heian Shrine, Kyoto. (Sekai Bunka) **36** *Story of Kitano Tenjin,* scroll, Kamakura period, Fletcher Fund, Metropolitan Museum of Art **37** *Story of Kitano Tenjin,* scroll, Kamakura period. Kitano Temmangu, Kyoto. (SB) **38** Irises at Heian Shrine, Kyoto. (Sekai Bunka) **38–39** Old Imperial Palace, Kyoto. (Sekai Bunka) **41** top, Kemari; bottom, Cockfight. Both from *Annual Functions,* scroll, 10–11th century. Both: Tanaka Chikayoshi, Tokyo (SB) **43** Enryaku-ji, Kyoto. (EB) **45** Wooden statue of Kukai, 9–10th century. Koyasan Reiho-kan, Wakayama (SB) **47** *Caricature of Birds and Beasts,* by Toba Sojo, scroll, 1053–1140. Kozan-ji, Kyoto (SB) **48** *The Tale of Genji,* scroll attributed to Fujiwari Takayoshi, 12th century. Tokugawa Art Museum, Nagoya (SB) **49** Manuscript of *The Tale of Genji.* Yomei Bunka, Kyoto (SB) **50** Amida Buddha, by Jocho, 11th century. Byodo-in, Kyoto (SB) **50–51** Phoenix Hall, Byodo-in, Kyoto. (Sekai Bunka)

CHAPTER III **53** Gyodo mask, from Toji-in, Kyoto. SAM **54–55** *Tale of the Heiji War,* scroll, 13th century. NM,T (SB) **57** Jakko-in, Kyoto (EB) **58–59** *Tale of the Heiji War,* scroll, 13th century. Museum of Fine Arts, Boston (SB) **62–63** top, Preparing fish; bottom: Eating rice. Both: *On Drink and Food,* scroll, 14th century. Both: Okura Shukokan Museum, Tokyo (SB) **64** top, Gilt wood Kannons, Sanjusangendo, Kyoto. (Sekai Bunka); bottom, Wooden statue of war god, 12th century. Kofuku-ji, Nara (SB) **65** Guardian statue, 7–8th century. Shin Yakushi-ji, Nara (SB) **66** Map by Francis & Shaw, Inc. **68–69** Samurai sword, Kamakura period (SB) **69** *The Mongol Invasion,* scroll, *c.* 1293. Imperial Household Agency, Kyoto (SB)

CHAPTER IV **71** Samurai battle mask, Momoyama period. SAM **72** Statue of Ashikaga Takauji, 14th century. Toji-in, Kyoto (SB) **73** Nanzen-ji, Kyoto. (Sekai Bunka) **75** *The Three Doctrines,* scroll attributed to Josetsu, 15th century. Ryosokuin, Kyoto (SB) **76** Kinkaku-ji, Kyoto. (EB) **78** *Mountain River,* scroll by Sesshu Toyo. Collection Mori Motomichi, Yamaguchi (SB) **79** *Landscape,* scroll by Sesshu Toyo, *c.* 1495. NM,T **80–81** Daitoko-ji, Kyoto. (Sekai Bunka) **83** Ginkaku-ji, Kyoto. (EB) **84** No robe, Edo period. (SB) **84–85** *Spectators at No Play,* screen, 16th century. Namban Art Museum, Hyogo (SB) **85** top, Three No Masks, Muromachi period; left and center, Kasuga Shrine, Seki, Gifu-ken (SB); right, NM,T (SB)

CHAPTER V **87** Lacquered wooden saddle, attributed to Kano Eitoku, 16th century. NM,T (SB) **88** *Scene of Country Life,* screen, 17th century, NM,T (SB) **89** *Imaginary Lion-like Beasts,* screen by Kano Eitoku, 16th century. Imperial Household Agency, Tokyo (SB) **91** Portrait of Oda Nobunaga, scroll, *c.* 1583. City Museum of Namban Art, Kobe **92–93** *Westerners Departing in a Sailing Ship,* screen, 17th century. City Museum of Namban Art, Kobe **96** *Osaka Castle,* screen. Mitsui Collection (SB) **97** Portrait of Toyotomi Hideyohsi, scroll, 1598. Kodai-ji, Kyoto (SB) **98–99** *Monkeys,* screen by Hasegawa Tohaku, 16th century. William Sturgis Bigelow Collection, Museum of Fine Arts, Boston **100–01** top, *Flower Viewing Party,* screen, 16th century. Uchu no Miya Art Museum, Osaka (SB); bottom, Sambo-in garden, Kyoto. (Sekai Bunka) **102** *Tiger,* screen attributed to Kano Eitoku, 16th century. Fenollosa-Weld Collection, Museum of Fine Arts, Boston. **104–05** Drawing room at Nijo Castle, Kyoto. (Sekai Bunka)

Index

NOTE: In standard Japanese usage, the surname precedes the given name. Thus Hasegawa Tohaku is indexed under Hasegawa. In the case of clan names, the given name is used for indexing. Fujiwara no Michinaga is therefore listed under Michinaga.